HOLY
MOMENTS

Activities for Teaching Children About Worship

Emily La Branche Delikat

Abingdon Press

Nashville

HOLY
MOMENTS

Activities for Teaching Children
About Worship

ISBN 9781501890895
PACP10572479-01

Writer: Emily La Branche Delikat
Production Editor: Rhonda Delph
Designer: Arvis Guilbault
Sign Language: Diana Magnuson;
Additional art © Abingdon Press.

Websites are constantly changing. Although the websites recommended in this resource were checked at the time this resource was developed, we recommend that you double-check all sites to verify that they are still live and that they are still suitable for children before doing the activity.

19 20 21 22 23 24 25 26 27 28—10 9 8 7 6 5 4 3 2 1
Printed in the United States of America

CONTENTS

1. Introduction

2. Entering

3. Proclaiming

4. Responding

CONTENTS

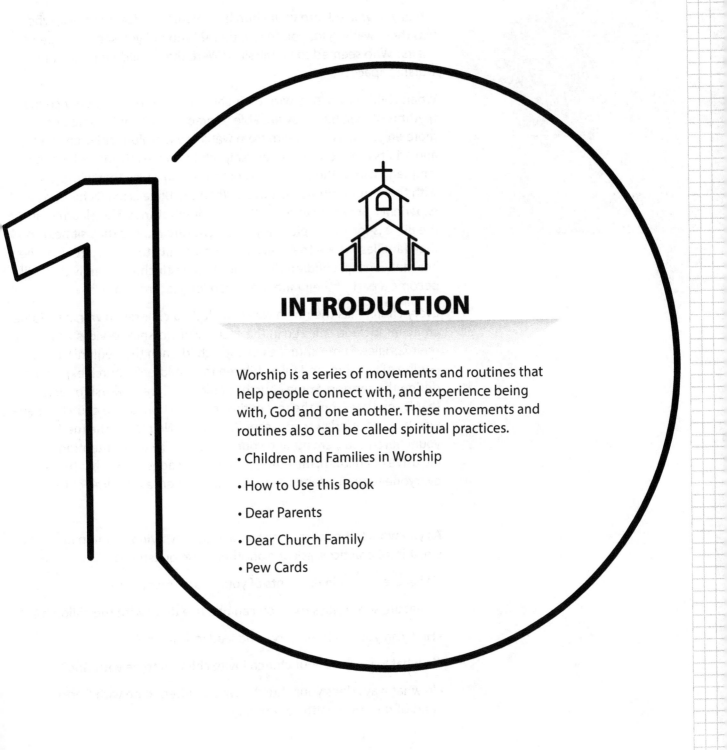

INTRODUCTION

Worship is a series of movements and routines that help people connect with, and experience being with, God and one another. These movements and routines also can be called spiritual practices.

- Children and Families in Worship
- How to Use this Book
- Dear Parents
- Dear Church Family
- Pew Cards

Children and Families in Worship

"Let the children come to me." — Jesus (Matthew 19)

When you walked into your church's worship service this week, who was there waiting for you to join them? Who did you see in the pews or chairs? Who seemed to be missing? Were there children present in your worship space?

When children worship with their church family, they experience the rhythms of worship. They are able to gradually become more and more engaged as they learn from watching the older children, youth, and adults around them. In worship, children are introduced to faith language within the context of community in a way that will grow with them throughout their lives. When the Bible is read, children experience Scripture as more than children's stories. They learn that the Bible is for all people. They hear Scripture read as they sit next to their families, where they have the opportunity to ask about what they hear. In worship, children sing songs with their church family that will become a part of their faith formation for years to come.

Every church has their own way of including children in worship. Some churches include children in the entirety of worship services with their families. Some churches include children in the beginning, and ending of worship, and take children to a children's church experience during the sermon. Some churches hold a children's worship service that is separate from the rest of the congregation. Some churches have worship and Sunday school simultaneously. No matter the method your church uses, encourage your church family to be intentionally inclusive of children. Including people of all ages in worship helps everyone to understand themselves and others as children of God.

As you work to be more intentional about involving children in worshipful practices, ask one another these questions:

• What are the main elements of your church's worship?

• What are some ways that you can practice them with the children?

• How can your children serve and lead in worship?

• In what ways does your church invite children to be with God?

• In what ways does your church invite children to be with God as a part of the larger faith community?

How to Use this Book

What is a Holy Moment?

Worship at church is a series of movements and routines that help people connect with, and experience being with, God and one another. These movements and routines also can be called spiritual practices, or Holy Moments. There are Holy Moments we use each time we worship together, such as singing, praying, or listening to a sermon. These practices have combined and developed over time into what we know as our worship liturgy*. You likely notice when one of the Holy Moments of your church's worship service has changed or been deleted.

How do Holy Moments help children and their families learn about worship?

When children experience Holy Moments with the congregation, those moments become a part of how they experience God and the family of God with whom they worship. Practicing the Holy Moment elements of worship in other relaxed environments can help children and families become more comfortable participating together.

In this book you will find a page for each Holy Moment that is found in a typical worship service. It contains at least one Holy Moment activity as well as information and inspiration for you as you prepare to lead the activity. These are activities that work well both with a group of children or an intergenerational group. Throughout the book you also will find *"Holy Moments at Home"* pages. These pages are great for reproducing and sharing with families. They include activities for families to do together that help to connect Holy Moments with daily life.

The word "liturgical" (liturgy) comes from the Greek word leitourgia, which means "the work of the people." You may hear the word "liturgy" used in reference to the order of worship in your church bulletin or in reference to the liturgical year. Worship is liturgy, the work of the people.

When and where can I use Holy Moment Activities?

• As an addition to your children's worship time each week

• As an addition to your Sunday-school classroom routine each week

• As an occasional addition to your children's ministry events when the Holy Moment matches the Bible story (This especially works well for special days and seasons, communion, and baptism.)

• As a children's sermon

• As an occasional substitute for a portion of the typical liturgy used in your church's service

• As a training tool for children who serve in worship

• As elements of an intergenerational worship service (pp. 79-80)

Dear Parents,

Thank you for taking us to church. We learn so much about God, ourselves, and the people around us when we go to worship. There are a few things we would like you to know.

- We know it is hard for you to take us to church on Sundays. It is a lot of work to get everyone ready and out the door. Thank you!

- We like to sing, listen, and pray with everyone. Being part of the church feels like being a part of a big family.

- We like to feel included in what is happening in worship. It helps when you show us what to do and how to participate.

- Sometimes worship is boring. Sometimes we don't understand what is happening, and sometimes we just aren't interested.

- Sometimes we just need to talk. When we have questions or have a problem, we may need to whisper to you or even step out of the room.

- We have lots of questions! If the question is complicated, it's OK to tell us that you need to answer after worship. Help us remember the questions we have by writing them down. We can look for answers together later. When you write our questions, we see that what we think and wonder about matters to you.

- We know that you and other people in the worship space are trying to pay attention to what is going on. We are, too. We don't want to be a distraction. Sometimes we listen better when we move our bodies. Coloring books and fidget toys really help. It may look like we aren't paying attention, but we are learning a lot!

Love, Your Children

Dear Church Family,

Thank you! Being part of the church feels like being part of a big family. We learn so much about God, ourselves, and the people around us when we go to worship. There are a few things we would like you to know.

- We like to sing, listen, and pray with everyone.

- We like to feel included in what is happening in worship. It helps when you show us what to do and how to participate.

- Kids can do a lot of things to help in worship! Some of us can be acolytes or read the Bible. Some of us can sing or dance. Some of us can even preach or tell a story!

- Sometimes worship is boring. Sometimes we don't understand what is happening, and sometimes we just aren't interested.

- Sometimes we need to talk. When we have questions or have a problem, we may need to whisper to you or even step out of the room.

- We know that you and the other people in the worship space are trying to pay attention to what is going on. We are, too. We don't want to be a distraction, But sometimes we listen better when we move our bodies. It may look like we aren't paying attention, but we are learning a lot.

- Our parents love us very much, and want us to learn about Jesus and about being a part of the church community. It is hard for them to take us to church sometimes. Please be kind and patient with them and with us.

- Sit with us in worship. We learn a lot about worship from our parents, but we learn a lot from you, too. You can help us find the right page in the hymnal or Bible. You can help us when we drop crayons on the floor. We might even let you color with us during the sermon. Do you listen better when you color, too?

Love, Your Children

Pew Cards

INSTRUCTIONS: Photocopy the cards on card stock, then cut out. On the back of each card, add information about your church and how children are invited to participate in worship. Printable mailing labels (2"-by-3") work great for conveniently adding this information. Place several cards in each pew along with crayons or worship bags. Periodically replace cards that have been colored and/or taken home.

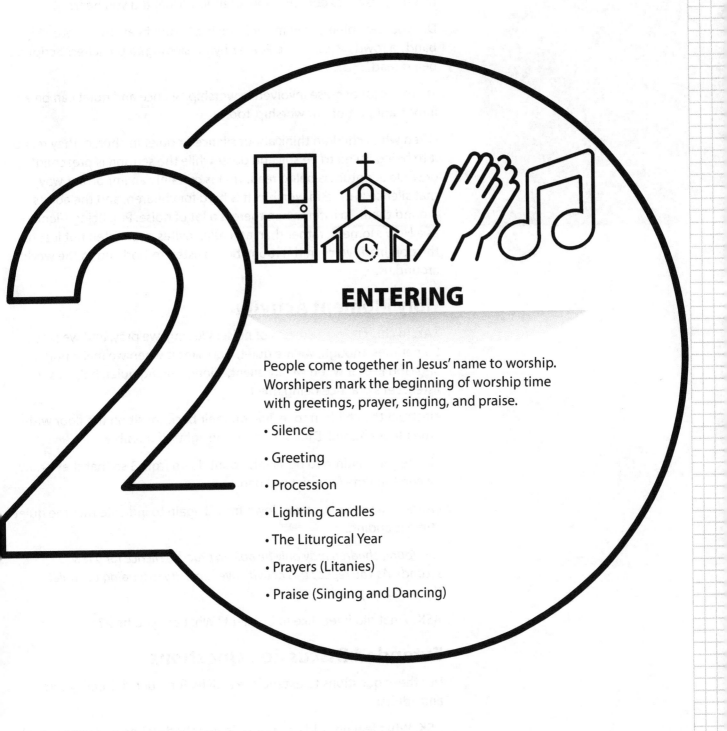

ENTERING

People come together in Jesus' name to worship. Worshipers mark the beginning of worship time with greetings, prayer, singing, and praise.

- Silence
- Greeting
- Procession
- Lighting Candles
- The Liturgical Year
- Prayers (Litanies)
- Praise (Singing and Dancing)

Silence

Preparing to Lead: Worship Sounds

What does worship sound like? Close your eyes and imagine the most recent worship experience you attended. What did you hear?

Did you hear pipe organ music? praying? drum beats from a worship band? a rowdy Passing the Peace? hymn singing? a preacher? Scripture being read?

There is *a lot* of noise involved in worship. Silence and quiet can be an important part of our worship, too.

Often when children think about silence or quiet in church, they relate it to being asked to be still and quiet while the sermon is preached or while Scripture is being read. That is certainly an important way that silence is used in worship. It is hard for children, and the adults around them, to listen when there is a lot of noise. Practicing silence as a Holy Moment, rather than as a rule, invites us to listen not just to the dominant voice in the room, but to listen to God and to the world around us.

Holy Moment Activity

SAY: In church we make lots of noise! We sing, we pray, and we play. Sometimes, though, we are quiet. God likes it when we make noise, and God likes it when we are silent. Silence, being quiet, helps us to listen. Let's practice being quiet.

- Instruct the children to recline on their backs or sit on the floor with their legs crossed. Dim or turn off the lights, if possible.

- Invite the children to be silent. Count down from 3 so that they know when the time for quiet will begin.

- After 5-10 seconds, count down from 3 again to indicate that the quiet time is ending.

TIP: *Young children may only be able to practice silence for a few seconds. As you repeat this activity over time, try extending the quiet time gradually.*

ASK: What did it feel like to be silent? What did you hear?

Extended Discussion Questions

Use these questions to extend the activity for older children, youth, and adults:

ASK: What feelings did you notice in your body when you were silent?

ASK: Why is being silent an important thing to practice?

Holy Moments at Home: Silence

Dear Parents and Caregivers,

We have been learning about practicing silence as a worshipful Holy Moment.

Often when children think about silence or being quiet in church, they relate it to being asked to be still and quiet while the sermon is preached or while Scripture is being read. That is certainly an important way that silence is used in worship. It is difficult for children, and the adults around them to listen when there is a lot of noise. Practicing silence as a Holy Moment rather than as a rule, invites us to listen not just to the dominant voice in the room, but to listen to God and to the world around us.

Try some of these activities as a family. How might practicing silence as a Holy Moment at Home help your family connect with God and one another?

Quiet Night

- Turn off all of the noise-making electronics, such as televisions, computers, and cell phones, for at least one hour.

- Spend time together doing something as a family, or do quiet activities individually.

Imagining Together

SAY: What does worship sound like? Close your eyes and imagine what it was like in worship when we were last at our church.

- Sit quietly for a few seconds.

SAY: Slowly open your eyes. What did you hear in your imagination?

- Discuss what you each imagined. To start the conversation, you may want to offer a suggestion such as singing, praying, or the sermon.

Practicing Purposeful Pause

- Practice taking turns speaking so that when one person finishes his or her thought, there is a second of silence before the next person speaks.

Silent-Listening Walk

- Go on a walk together. Try staying silent as you move together, even if only for a few moment at a time.

- Stop occasionally to have conversations about what you heard and thought about during the silence.

**Be still before the LORD, and wait for him.
(Psalm 37:7a)**

Recommended Resources for the Whole Family

The Quiet Book, Deborah Underwood (Picture Book - ages 3+)

A Quiet Place, Douglas Wood (Picture Book - ages 3+)

Silence, Lemniscates (Picture Book - ages 3+)

The Power of Silence, Neal Gittleman (TEDx Talk Video - appropriate for all ages but most interesting for 10+)
    https://youtube.com/watch?v=ec9GyxEUGec

Absolute Silence, CBS and Jeff Glor (News Segment Video - appropriate for all ages)
    https://youtube.com/watch?v=/i_Rl98sqz6o

Dialogues with Silence: Prayers and Drawings, Thomas Merton (Book - adults)

Greeting

Preparing to Lead: Hello, Friends!

You are walking down the street or a hallway and notice someone coming toward you. The person may be a friend or may be a stranger. What do you imagine will happen? Often you will experience an exchange like this: "Hello, how are you?" "Doing well, and you?" "Well, thanks!" As you prepare to participate in the Holy Moment of greeting, think about these questions: Why do we greet one another? What are some of the verbal and non-verbal ways we greet one another? How do people in your church greet one another during worship?

Holy Moment Activity

SAY: When we gather together for worship, we greet one another in the name of Jesus. When we greet one another at the beginning of worship, we show that we love and care for one another. When you greet a neighbor and they greet you in return, it reminds you both that you are part of the same family of God. One greeting we use in worship is when the pastor or leader says, "The Lord be with you." Do you know what the congregation says in response? ("And also with you.")

- Practice the greeting together several times. If time and interest allow, give each child an opportunity to begin the greeting by saying, "The Lord be with you."

Holy Moment Activity

Supplies: crayons, markers, poster board

- Place poster board on a table. Write the word *WELCOME!* in large letters in the center.

- Invite the children to color and draw around the word to create a colorful welcome poster.

- Hang the welcome poster where people entering your worship space will see it, and feel welcomed.

Extended Discussion Questions

Use these questions to extend the activity for older children, youth, and adults:

ASK: Why do we welcome one another?

ASK: How does it feel to be welcomed? How does it feel to welcome others?

Procession

Preparing to Lead: Here Comes the Procession

It is almost time for worship to begin and the pastor, choir, acolytes, and others are lining up at the back of the sanctuary. They are preparing to begin the processional. Some churches have a procession, and some do not. Some have people come in during the first hymn or an instrumental offering, and some have a quiet procession before worship begins. Some churches have only the pastor enter the sanctuary from the back, while others have a large group of people carry in a variety of symbols of God's presence.

Use this Holy Moment for talking about how processions work in your church. The activity describes the people and items in a fairly typical protestant procession. Your church may not use every element. If you do not have a procession, talk about how the worship service begins in your church.

Holy Moment Activity

Supplies: Bible, battery-operated candles or unlit candlelighters, cross

SAY: In many churches, when a worship service begins, some very special items are brought into the worship space. This time is called the Procession. It is like a small parade. First, a cross is brought in. The person who brings in the cross is called a "crucifer" (CROO si fur). Then the acolytes bring in the candlelighters. Finally, the Bible is brought in and placed at the pulpit. The pastors, worship helpers, and sometimes the choir members follow the cross, the light, and the Bible. Processions help us to focus on coming into the worship space to worship God. It also helps us remember how important Jesus, light, and Scripture are to our worship. Let's have our own procession.

- Invite a child to carry a cross (it does not have to be large.)

- Invite two children to carry battery-operated candles or unlit candlelighters like those used in worship.

- Invite a child to carry a Bible.

- Invite the remaining children to line up behind the Bible carrier. They will be the ministers and choir members.

- Direct the children to line up at the door behind the child with the cross.

- Play music or sing a song.

- Encourage the children to walk in a procession around the room.

Extended Discussion Questions

Use these questions to extend the activity for older children, youth, and adults:

ASK: Have you ever been an acolyte or crucifer? What did it feel like?

ASK: Why do people serve at the beginning of worship, carrying into the sanctuary things that remind us of God?

Lighting Candles

Preparing to Lead: Bringing in the Light

While teaching people in the temple, Jesus said, "I am the light of the world. Whoever follows me won't walk in darkness but will have the light of life" (John 8:12).

One of my favorite symbols in a worship space is a candle or set of candles. As a child I would watch the candlelight flicker as I listened to the sermon or sang and prayed along with my family and friends. I still think of the presence of God when I watch the flame of a lit candle, smell the distinct smell of burning wax, or feel the warmth of candlelight.

As you prepare to lead this activity, sit in a quiet place. Light a candle and place it on a stable surface in front of you. Take a deep breath. Pay attention to what you feel, see, hear, and smell. Read aloud John 8:12, "I am the light of the world. Whoever follows me won't walk in darkness but will have the light of life."

Holy Moment Activity

Supplies: candles, battery-operated candles (optional), long-handled lighter

SAY: In many churches, people light candles at the beginning of the worship service. Sometimes children are the ones who light the candles. Children who light the candles are called acolytes. The lighted candles remind us that God is with us when we worship. We know that God is always with us; the candles are something beautiful to help remind us. Let's light candles and keep them lit during our time together.

• Real candles placed in a safe location (where they won't get knocked over) are ideal. Battery-powered candles are non-flame alternatives.

• Light, or have a child help you light, the candles.

PRAY: Thank you, God, for always being with us, and for these candles that remind us. Amen.

Extended Discussion Questions

Use these questions to extend the activity for older children, youth, and adults:

ASK: What do think of when you see or imagine candlelight? When are some other times when you use candles?

ASK: Why are lit candles used as a symbol for God's presence? How do they remind us of Jesus?

God Is with Us

The symbols in our worship space remind us that God is with us. In the box below, draw another symbol from our worship space that reminds you of God's presence.

HOLY MOMENTS: Activities for Teaching Children About Worship

Holy Moments at Home: Beginning Worship

Dear Parents and Caregivers,

Worship at church is a series of movements and routines that help people connect with and experience being with God and one another. These movements and routines also can be called spiritual practices. Each spiritual practice is important. Even our greeting and entering rituals help us to connect.

A typical worship service begins with a greeting and a song. Many churches also light candles, and some have a procession. These spiritual practices help to prepare our hearts and minds for worship. Next time you are in worship together as a family, pay special attention to the ways that the beginning moments of the service help to prepare you for what is to come.

God is with Us Walk

SAY: When we go to church, we see lots of signs that God is with us. We see beautiful windows, crosses, and candles. What else do we see at church that reminds us of God?

God isn't just with us at church. God is with us everywhere we go.

- Go on a walk together. Look for signs that God is with you.
- Point out God's beautiful creation, and thank God for it.

Candlelight Dinner

SAY: In worship we light candles to remind us that God is with us. God is always with us. Let's light candles and eat dinner by candlelight.

- Light candles and place them on the table. If real candles can't be used safely, use battery-operated candles.

ASK: How do the candles remind you of God?

- Does dinner feel different with candlelight?

Welcome Mat

- Create or purchase a new welcome mat or sign for your home. What should it say?

The Lord be with You

- Try greeting one another with "The Lord be with you." Respond with, "And also with you."

Let's enter God's dwelling place; let's worship at the place God rests his feet! (Psalm 132:7)

Recommended Resources for the Whole Family

Maybe God Is Like That Too, Jennifer Grant (Picture Book - ages 4+)

A Church for All, Gayle E. Pitman (Picture Book - ages 3+; includes inclusive language and images)

This is the Church, Sarah Raymond Cunningham (Picture Book - ages 3+)

Candles, Discipleship Ministries (Chuck Knows Church Video - appropriate for all ages but most interesting for 10+) https://chuckknowschurch.com/archive/17candles

The Sign of the Fish, Discipleship Ministries (Chuck Knows Church Video - appropriate for all ages but most interesting for 10+) https://chuckknowschurch.com/archive/3sign-fish

The Liturgical Year

Preparing to Lead: Liturgical

Each New Year's Eve, as the clock strikes midnight and time moves into January 1st, we celebrate the birth of a brand new year. We start new calendars and journals. We celebrate all of the amazing possibilities a new year brings. We take time to remember Paul's words in 2 Corinthians 5:17b, "The old things have gone away, and look, new things have arrived!" What is it about the ritual marking of the passage of time through celebrations that helps us feel renewed, energized, and hopeful?

While people mark the passage of time by days, months, weather seasons, and years, Christians also mark time by the seasons of faith and Christian tradition using a special calendar called a *"liturgical calendar."* The word *"liturgical"* (liturgy) comes from the Greek word *leitourgia,* which means "the work of the people." You also may hear the word "liturgy" used in reference to the order of worship in your church bulletin. Worship is liturgy, the work of the people.

The liturgical year is broken into seven parts, each distinguished by using one of four colors.

- The new year begins with the season of Advent (purple.) Advent begins four Sundays before Christmas.

- The Christmas season follows (white). Christmas includes the twelve days from Christmas Eve (December 24) through Epiphany (January 6).

- Then comes the first Ordinary Time (green), which lasts until the season of Lent.

- Lent (purple) begins on Ash Wednesday and lasts until Easter.

- The Easter (white) season is 50 days long. It begins on the first Sunday after the first full moon after March 21.

- The Day of Pentecost (red) is the final day of the Easter season.

- Finally, the second Ordinary Time (green) begins, and the season lasts until Advent begins again.

Holy Moment Activity

Supplies: crayons

- Photocopy "The Liturgical Calendar" (p. 20), one per child.

- Give each child a copy of "The Liturgical Calendar."

- Show the children each season on the calendar, and invite them to color each one appropriately.

OPTION: Help the children find and mark other important days, such as their birthdays.

A Year of Worship: The Liturgical Calendar

INSTRUCTIONS: We use colors to remind us of seasons and special days. Our preparing seasons, Advent and Lent, are purple. The seasons of Christmas and Easter are white. Ordinary Time is green; that is what we call the time between the Christmas and Easter cycles. Read and color the calendar. What is your favorite season of our worship year? When are other special days in your family? What season are they in?

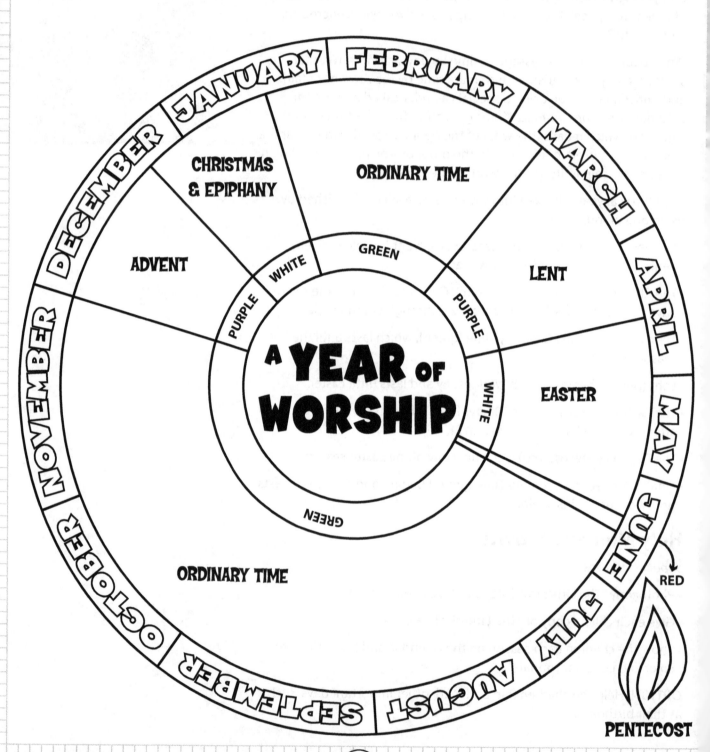

Prayers (Litanies)

Preparing to Lead: I Pray, We Pray

Praying during the beginning part of the worship service is a sign that we are entering into a time spent with God. As a community, one kind of prayer used during this time is called a *litany*. A litany is a call and response between a leader and the larger group. Usually the leader will have a longer statement or prayer, while the congregation or group will have a shorter repeated response. As you prepare to lead this Holy Moment, think about these questions:

• When have you experienced a litany in worship? What was the response said by the congregation? Was it a litany of praise, confession, or supplication (asking for something)?

Holy Moment Activity

Supplies: pencils or markers, poster board

SAY: One way that we pray together in worship is by reading a litany. A litany is a call and response. The leader says something, then the congregation responds together by saying a repeated phrase. Sometimes the litany is about praising God, sometimes it is about confessing that we need forgiveness, and sometimes it is about asking God to be with us and help us. Today let's write our own litany of praise to God about what we are thankful for.

• Write the phrase "We thank you, God" on poster board and display.

• Read the phrase to the children and practice repeating it together.

• Invite the children to name things and people they are thankful for. Write each thing or person on the poster board.

• When every child has had an opportunity to name at least one person or thing, invite the children to pray with you. Read each suggested thing or person, pausing after each one to respond with the children, "We thank you, God."

• End the prayer by saying together "Amen."

OPTION: With the children's permission, share the prayer with the rest of the congregation by hanging the poster board where others in the congregation can view it, copying the litany for use in worship, or by taking a picture of the poster board and sharing it digitally.

Holy Moment Activity

Supplies: crayons

• Photocopy "So Many Ways to Pray" (p. 24), one per child.

• Give each child a copy of "So Many Ways to Pray."

• Assist the children in folding the pages into books, then let them color the pictures.

• Read the books together.

Extended Discussion Questions

Use these questions to extend the activity for older children, youth, and adults:

ASK: How did it feel to respond in chorus with the congregation?

ASK: How is praying a written prayer together the same as praying alone or extemporaneously (off the top of your head)? How is it different?

Praise (Singing and Dancing)

Preparing to Lead: Praise God!

How do you show your appreciation and love for others? How do you show your love and appreciation for God? Worshiping at church is a time when people who love God share their appreciation for God together in praise. Praise can look, sound, and feel different. Sometimes praise is quiet and sometimes it is loud. Sometimes praise is busy and moving, and sometimes it is still.

What is praise like in your church's worship? Does praise look the same in the sanctuary as it does in the Sunday-school classroom? Why or why not?

Holy Moment Activity

SAY: Praise is a word that means showing how much we love, like, or admire someone. There are lots of ways to praise God. We do a lot of singing during our worship services. We can even worship through dance! Let's sing and dance together.

• Sing "Praise the Lord" (p. 23).

• Point to and wiggle each body part as it is mentioned in the song.

Holy Moment Activity

Supplies: hymnals

SAY: One of the ways we praise God when we worship is by singing songs together. Sometimes we sing out of books called hymnals.

• Distribute hymnals for children to explore.

• Open the hymnal to any hymn. Point out the features of the page to the children. Show the hymn numbers, titles, notes, and verses.

• Choose a hymn of praise familiar to the children and sing it together.

Holy Moment Activity

Supplies: hymnals

SAY: We can praise God with our voices and our whole bodies!

• Sing together "I Can Praise God" (p. 23).

• Invite the children to work together to create movements to go with the song.

• Sing and move together.

Songs

"Praise the Lord"
(Tune: Head, Shoulders, Knees, and Toes)

Head, shoulders, knees, and toes, knees and toes.
Head, shoulders, knees, and toes, knees and toes.
My whole body can praise the Lord!
Head, shoulders, knees, and toes, knees and toes.
Eyes, ears, mouth, and nose, mouth and nose.
Eyes, ears, mouth, and nose, mouth and nose.
My whole body can praise the Lord!
Eyes, ears, mouth and nose, mouth and nose.

"Forgiveness"
(Tune: "Are You Sleeping?")

I am sorry. I am sorry.
You're my friend. You're my friend.
I am very sorry. I made a mistake.
I love you. I love you.

I forgive you. I forgive you.
You're my friend. You're my friend.
You said that you are sorry. You made a mistake.
I love you. I love you.

"I Can Praise God"
(Tune: "Pop Goes the Weasel")

I can praise God all day long!
I can sing and dance.
I can praise God all day long.
Praise God with music.
I will praise God all day long!
I will sing and dance.
I will praise God all day long.
Praise God with music.

"I Can Talk to God"
(Tune: "The Farmer in the Dell")

I can talk to God.
I can talk to God.
I can talk to God each day.
God hears me when I pray.

"Be Strong: Psalm 27:14"
(Tune: "The Bear Went Over the Mountain")

Be strong! Let your heart take courage!
Be strong! Let your heart take courage!
Be strong! Let your heart take courage
and hope in the LORD!

"Every Time I Feel the Spirit"
(Tune: Public Domain)

Every time I feel the Spirit
moving in my heart, I will pray.
Yes, every time I feel the Spirit
moving in my heart, I will pray.

"Every Time I Feel the Spirit," words: Public Domain Tune: The tune can be found in The United Methodist Hymnal #404 or online. "Praise the Lord," words adapted by Emily Delikat; "I Can Praise God," "Be Strong," and "Forgiveness," are selections from Piggyback Psalms: 100+ Bible Songs to Tunes You Know.
Copyright © 2018 by Abingdon Press. All rights reserved. Used by permission.

So Many Ways to Pray

I can stand,
raise my arms,
and smile
with delight.

I can kneel,
fold my hands,
and shut my
eyes tight.

There are
so many ways
to pray!

There are
so many ways
to pray!

HOLY MOMENTS: Activities for
Teaching Children About Worship

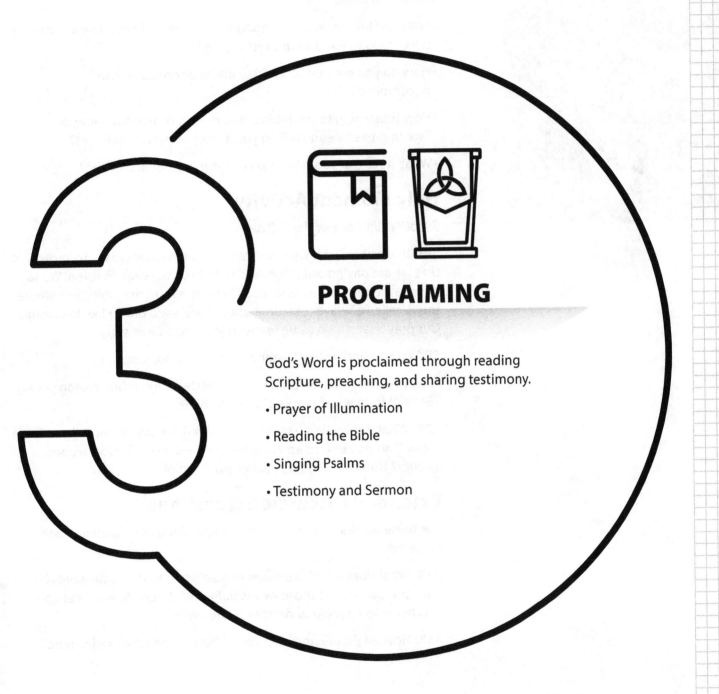

PROCLAIMING

God's Word is proclaimed through reading Scripture, preaching, and sharing testimony.

- Prayer of Illumination
- Reading the Bible
- Singing Psalms
- Testimony and Sermon

Prayer of Illumination

Preparing to Lead: Listening

Think about these questions as you prepare for leading this Holy Moment activity:

- What are the qualities of a good listener? How do you know someone is listening to you and understanding?

- How do you prepare to listen to information that is hard or complicated?

- How is listening to the Bible being read in church the same as listening to someone telling you a story? How is it different?

- What steps can you take to be a better listener in worship?

Holy Moment Activity

Supplies: Bible or Storybook Bible

SAY: In worship time, we have a special prayer that we say to show God that we are paying attention, and to help us be ready to listen. We say this prayer before someone reads Scripture from the Bible. Sometimes this is called a "Prayer of Illumination." I will say a prayer like that today. Our prayer is to help us be ready to listen to a Bible story.

PRAY: Dear God, help us listen and understand. Amen.

- Read 1 Samuel 3:1-20 from the Bible, or the story of God calling young Samuel from your favorite storybook Bible.

ASK: What did you learn about God from this story? What did you learn about listening to God and one another? How was Samuel a good listener? How did Samuel improve his listening?

Extended Discussion Questions

Use these questions to extend the activity for older children, youth, and adults:

ASK: What does it feel like when people listen to the same words being said, but understand those words differently? How do you treat one another when people understand differently?

ASK: How might praying help you to better listen and understand?

Prayer of Illumination

Dear **God**, **Help me listen** and **understand**. Amen.

God
Point the index finger of your right hand, with the other fingers curled down. Bring the hand down in front of your face as if you are drawing a shepherd's crook. Open the palm as you bring your hand down. End with your hand flat and your palm facing left.

Help
Close your left hand into a fist with your thumb pointing up. Place your left hand on top of your open right hand, and lift both hands up.

I (me)
Point to yourself.

Listen
Place your right hand next to your head with your thumb touching your ear and your fingers curled down. Curl and uncurl your index and middle fingers.

Understand
Hold your loosely closed right hand near your forehead. Then point your index finger up with a flicking motion.

Reading the Bible

Preparing to Lead: God's Word

There are many ways that God speaks to us. God speaks through nature, through our hearts and minds, and through the words of others. God speaks to us through the Bible, and especially through the words and actions of Jesus. During worship we interact with the Bible by listening to, reading, and singing Scripture. We also interact with the Bible through listening to others share their understanding and experience of Scripture. Sometimes we even share our own understanding and experience with others within the worship service.

To prepare to lead this Holy Moment Activity, spend some time with your Bible. Refamiliarize yourself with the Bible's structure as a library of books.

Holy Moment Activity

Supplies: Bible, bookmarks

- Prepare a Bible by using four bookmarks (or a bookmark with four ribbons) to mark the Old Testament, Psalms, Gospels, and New Testament.

SAY: Reading Scripture, or words from the Bible, is a very important part of our worship time. The Bible is one of the many ways that God speaks to us. Before the preacher preaches a sermon, someone will read from the Bible. He or she usually reads the story that the preacher will talk about in his or her sermon. In some churches, more than one Scripture passage is read each week. Some churches read Scripture from both the Old Testament and New Testament. Some churches add a psalm and a reading from one of the four Gospels.

- Display a Bible. Point out the Old and New Testaments, then the Psalms and Gospels.

SAY: When the reader is finished, he or she will sometimes say, "The Word of God for the people of God." Then everyone responds with "Thanks be to God." Let's try that. I will say "The Word of God for the people of God." You say, "Thanks be to God."

"The Word of God for the people of God." ***"Thanks be to God."***

Listen to this Scripture: This is a New Testament reading from 2 Timothy, chapter 3, verses 15 through 17.

"Since childhood you have known the holy scriptures that help you to be wise in a way that leads to salvation through faith that is in Christ Jesus. Every scripture is inspired by God and is useful for teaching, for showing mistakes, for correcting, and for training character, so that the person who belongs to God can be equipped to do everything that is good."

"This is the word of God for the people of God." ***"Thanks be to God. Amen."***

Singing Psalms

Preparing to Lead: Singing Scripture

The Book of Psalms in the Bible is a book of poetry and songs that reflect the wide range of emotions and experiences of the people of God. Some are full of praise and happiness. Others are full of sadness and anger. There are many ways to use psalms in worship. Psalms can be prayed, read, or sung.

To prepare to lead this Holy Moment, choose a psalm from the Bible. Slowly read it to yourself. Think about how the psalmist, or writer, was feeling. Can you relate? Think about the way the psalmist responded to his or her thoughts and feelings. Can you relate? How might writing songs and poems like the psalmist be helpful in your relationship to God and to others?

How does your church use psalms in worship?

Holy Moment Activity

Supplies: Bible, bookmarks

- Prepare a Bible by using four bookmarks (or a bookmark with four ribbons) to mark the Old Testament, Psalms, Gospels, and New Testament.

SAY: During worship we read Scripture, or words from the Bible. Sometimes we read from the Old Testament, and sometimes we read from the New Testament. One of the Books in the Old Testament is called the Book of Psalms. It is a book of poetry and songs. When we read Psalms, sometimes we read it with our speaking voices, sometimes with our singing voices, and sometimes with both.

- Display a Bible. Point out the Old and New Testaments, then Psalms.

- Turn to Psalm 27.

SAY: Let's read and sing Psalm 27 together. I will read a few verses, then we will sing a chorus.

- Sing the chorus "Be Strong" (p. 23) to the tune of "The Bear Went Over the Mountain." Sing it together several times.

- Read Psalm 27 aloud. Pause to sing the chorus "Be Strong" together after verses 1, 6, 9, 13, and 14.

Extended Discussion Questions

Use these questions to extend the activity for older children, youth, and adults:

ASK: What feelings did you hear in the psalmist's words? Have you ever felt that way?

ASK: Why do you imagine we sing psalms together instead of just listening or reading?

Holy Moments at Home: Reading the Bible

Dear Parents and Caregivers,

We have been learning about reading and listening to the Bible, or Scripture, in worship. We have learned that the Bible is not only a book, but a whole library of books. These books are divided into the Old Testament and the New Testament. We learned that the Bible includes the four Books about Jesus called Gospels and a Book of songs and poetry called Psalms. We read and listen to the Bible at church because the Bible is the story of God and God's people.

Experience and explore the story of God and God's people together by reading and listening to the Bible at home. You may choose to read directly from a Bible or from a Bible storybook. The Common English Bible (CEB) is a great translation to begin with.

Help Me Listen

- Sit together and have a meal.

SAY: In worship at church we say a prayer before we listen to someone read the Bible. We ask God to help us listen and understand. Sometimes listening to and understanding one another is hard. Let's say a prayer to thank God for our food, but also to ask God to help us listen and understand one another.

PRAY: Dear God, thank you for this food and for this time together. Please be with us as we share this meal. Help us to listen and understand one another.

- Throughout the meal, take turns sharing about how the day went and how you are feeling.

Illustrating God's Word

Read the story from the Bible or a Bible storybook about Jesus calming a storm (Mark 4:35-41).

- Invite each family member to illustrate the story with pencils, crayons, or markers.

- Share and talk about each person's illustration. How are they the same? How are they different?

Remember and Praise

Read Psalm 117 together, and write it on poster board. Hang it on a wall where the whole family can see it.

- Set a goal to memorize the psalm as a family.

- Memorize the psalm, then celebrate as a family.

Your word is a lamp before my feet and a light for my journey. (Psalm 119:105)

Recommended Resources for the Whole Family

CEB Deep Blue Kids Bible (Bible - ages 7-12)

Bible Basics Storybook, Brittany Sky (Bible Storybook- ages 3+)

Deep Blue Kids Bible Dictionary (Bible Dictionary - ages 5+)

Learning to Use My Bible Student Guide, Abingdon Press (Workbook - ages 7-12)

Learning to Study The Bible Participant Book, L.J. Zimmerman (Workbook - adult)

Piggyback Psalms: 100+ Bible Songs to Tunes You Know, Emily La Branche Delikat (Songbook - all ages)

Psalms of Praise: A Movement Primer, Danielle Hitchen (Board Book - ages 0-3)

Making Sense of the Bible: Rediscovering the Power of Scripture Today, Adam Hamilton (Book - adult)

Telling God's Story: A Parent's Guide to Teaching the Bible, Peter Enns (Book - adult)

Testimony and Sermon

Preparing to Lead: Tell Me About It

What is the most important and meaningful part of a church worship service for you? The music? The prayers? For many, it is the sermon that is the main attraction. How does the sermon make you feel? Do you look forward to hearing the pastor, or another person, preach about the Scripture passage?

For children, the sermon time can be difficult. Not only is it the longest stretch of the worship service when they must be quiet, the pastor often doesn't seem to be talking to them. Often churches will have the children leave the sanctuary during this time, so they can receive teaching on their level in another space. Some provide coloring pages, puzzles, or worship bags for the children to use. On page 34 you will find a "Sermon Notes" page that you may photocopy and share with your families. Older children may find writing or drawing their thoughts and questions to be a helpful way to interact with the sermon. Though a whispered question during the sermon should not be discouraged, children often have questions that are too involved to lean over and whisper. The Family Talk Cards reproducible (p. 33) are also a great way to encourage your families to talk about God together at home.

This Holy Moment is intended to help children understand the purpose of the sermon time, and to invite them into the practice of sharing their thoughts on Scripture and God. They will learn both about preaching and about sharing a testimony.

Holy Moment Activity

SAY: When we come together to worship, we sing, pray, and listen. After someone reads words from the Bible, usually our pastor or another friend stands up and tells us more about what we heard. We call that time the "sermon." The person who is preaching shares his or her thoughts about how the Bible connects to our lives. Sometimes people also share testimonies in worship. A testimony is a story someone shares about when he or she experienced God. While not everyone feels called by God to stand in the pulpit to preach, anyone can preach a sermon or share a testimony. You can share your thoughts on the Bible and share how you have experienced God, too.

• Invite the children to sit in a circle and ask one of the questions below. Give them a moment to think quietly. Then invite them to share their thoughts one at a time. Continue until each child who would like to share has done so. Respect and honor those children who do not wish to speak by allowing them to make that choice.

ASK: What is your favorite Bible story? Why?

ASK: Did anything happen this week that made you feel happy or excited? Tell us about it.

Holy Moments at Home: Testimony and Sermon

Dear Parents and Caregivers,

What is the most important and meaningful part of a church worship service for you? The music? The prayers? For many, it is the sermon that is the main attraction. How does the sermon make you feel? Do you look forward to hearing the pastor, or another person, preach about the Scripture passage? Do you sometimes find the sermon time to be confusing?

For children, the sermon time can be difficult. Not only is it the longest stretch of the worship service when they must be quiet, the pastor often doesn't seem to be talking to them. Older children may find writing or drawing their thoughts and questions to be a helpful way to interact with the sermon. Though a whispered question during the sermon should not be discouraged, children often have questions that are too involved to lean over and whisper. Younger children may find that drawing pictures, making shapes out of chenille stems, or playing with a fidget toy helps them to listen and be present.

Family Talk	Preacher Play
• Turn off all of the noise-making electronics, such as televisions, computers, and cell phones, for at least one hour. • Sit together over dinner or in another space and take turns sharing about your day. **ASK:** What was your favorite things that happened today? **ASK:** Did anything happen today that made you feel sad or angry? What did you do?	Set a shelf, side table, or other tall but sturdy piece of furniture at the front of the room as a pretend pulpit. Set up chairs, couches, or blankets facing the pretend pulpit. • If your pastor wears a robe, stole, or clergy collar, make available fabric scraps that can be used for dress-up play. • Take turns pretending to be the preacher or a person in the congregation.
Dinner Guest	**Wondering Together**
Invite your pastor to share a meal with your family. • Ask your pastor to share about how she or he decided to become a preacher. • Invite the children to ask the pastor questions about his or her job.	Read a story from a Bible storybook together. • Take some time to wonder together about what the story means. • If there are questions to wonder about included in the storybook, answer those together.

Right away, he began to preach about Jesus in the synagogues. "He is God's Son," he declared. (Acts 9:20)

Recommended Resources for the Whole Family

• *Say Something,* Peter H. Reynolds (Picture Book - ages 4+)

• *Rufus the Writer,* Elizabeth Bram (Picture Book - ages 4+)

• *Sacred Stories of Ordinary Families: Living the Faith in Daily Life,* Diana R. Garland (Book - adult)

• *Deep Blue Bible Storybook Activity Bulletin Book,* Abingdon Press (Worship Bulletins - ages 4-7)

Family Talk Cards

INSTRUCTIONS: Photocopy the cards on card stock, and cut them out. Use an awl or paper punch to make a hole in the top left corner of each card. Stack the cards, then use a binder ring or ribbon to connect them. Read through the questions together.

Place the cards on a table wherever your family gathers. Use them as prompts for family discussion.

OPTION: Work together as a family to add an additional question to the back of each card.

FAMILY TALK

What was your favorite thing that happened today?

Did anything happen today that made you feel sad or angry?

What did you do?

Did anything happen today that made you feel happy or excited?

What did you do?

Where did you see God's creation today?

Did you help someone today?

Did someone help you?

What do you hope for?

How can we pray for one another?

I like you because...

I like me because...

HOLY MOMENTS: Activities for Teaching Children About Worship

Sermon Notes

Date:_____

The preacher's name:_____

Sermon Title:_____

The Bible story came from...

Book:

Chapter:

Verses:

I learned:
_____
_____
_____
_____
_____
_____

During the sermon, I thought about...
(write or draw)

I want to learn more about:
_____
_____
_____
_____
_____
_____
_____
_____

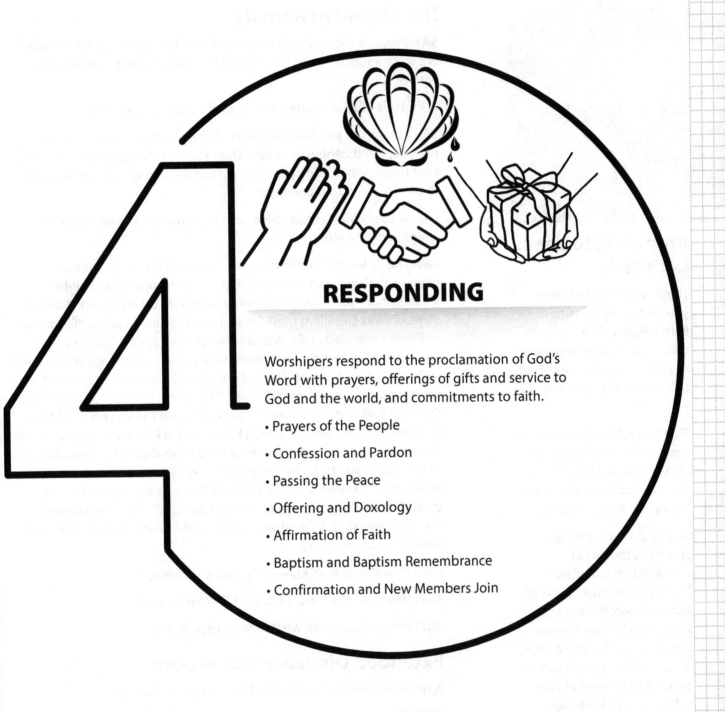

4 RESPONDING

Worshipers respond to the proclamation of God's Word with prayers, offerings of gifts and service to God and the world, and commitments to faith.

- Prayers of the People
- Confession and Pardon
- Passing the Peace
- Offering and Doxology
- Affirmation of Faith
- Baptism and Baptism Remembrance
- Confirmation and New Members Join

Prayers of the People (Conversation

Preparing to Lead: Let's Talk

Think about the last time you had a conversation with a friend. What did the conversation look and sound like? What did the two of you talk about? How did it make you feel?

Think about the last time you prayed. What did the prayer look and sound like? What did you and God talk about? How did it make you feel?

Maybe prayer looks like spending the day in conversation with God. There are two main parts of conversation, talking and listening. The same is true about prayer. We often focus on the talking part. It can be hard to understand the listening part. What does it mean to listen when we pray? How do we listen to God? Think about all of these things as you prepare for leading this Holy Moment.

Holy Moment Activity

Sing together "I Can Talk to God" (p. 23). Sing the song several times.

Holy Moment Activity

SAY: Prayer is like having a conversation with God. In the Bible there is a story about a young boy named Samuel who had a conversation with God.

• Display a Bible and point out Samuel's story in 1 Samuel 3:1-21.

SAY: Let me tell you Samuel's story. When you hear *"Samuel, Samuel,"* put your hand behind your ear. When you hear *"Go back to bed,"* shake your finger. When you hear *"Your servant is listening,"* raise your hands to the sky, with your palms up.

• Allow the children to practice each movement a few times before beginning the story.

SAY: The little boy Samuel grew and grew. He learned all about praying, praising, and serving God from Eli the priest. One night while Samuel was sleeping, a sound woke him up. He heard, *"Samuel, Samuel!"* Was Eli calling him? Samuel went to Eli and asked, "Eli, did you call me?" Eli replied, "I did not call you. *Go back to bed."* Samuel went back to bed and fell asleep. Before long, he was woken again by a voice saying, *"Samuel, Samuel!"* Samuel got up and went to Eli again and asked, "Eli, did you call me?" Eli said, "No. *Go back to bed."* So Samuel did. Once Samuel had fallen asleep again, he heard the voice a third time: *"Samuel, Samuel!"* Samuel said, "I know I heard Eli call me." Samuel went to see Eli. "I did not call you. It must have been God calling you. *Go back to bed.* When you hear the voice again, say 'Speak, Lord. Your servant is listening.'"* Samuel went back to bed. Within a short time, he woke up and heard the voice again: *"Samuel, Samuel!"* This time, knowing it was God speaking, Samuel said, *"Speak, Lord. Your servant is listening."* Samuel listened to God.

ASK: How did Samuel know that God was calling him?

ASK: Have you ever heard from God? What was it like?

ASK: How is prayer like what Samuel experienced?

Extended Discussion Questions

ASK: How do we know that God hears us when we pray?

ASK: What are some of the ways we hear God's voice?

Prayers of the People (Intercessary)

Preparing to Lead: You'll Be In My Prayers

A friend or family member tells you that they are not feeling well or that something bad has happened to them. What is your response? Perhaps you say, "I'm so sorry! I will keep you in my prayers." A church family member tells you that they are going to be having some medical tests next week. What is your response? Maybe you say, "I hope the tests go well. I will keep you in my prayers."

When we worship together we often pray for people in our church, communities, and world. These prayers are called intercessory prayers. Intercession is praying for God's intervention in the lives of those we love.

Think about these questions as you prepare to lead this Holy Moment Activity: Why do we pray for one another? How does it feel to know that someone is praying for you? How does it feel when what you prayed for happens? How does it feel when what you prayed for does not happen?

Holy Moment Activity

SAY: There are many reasons why we pray. Sometimes we pray to say "Thank you" to God. Sometimes we pray to tell God that we love God. Sometimes we pray for something we need or want. Sometimes we pray for something someone else needs or wants.

Today for our prayer time, we will pray for someone we love. We will take turns saying who we would like to pray for. After each name we will say "Lord, hear our prayer." We know that God always listen to our prayers.

- Give each child an opportunity to mention who he or she would like to pray for.

- After each name, say with the children, ***"Lord, hear our prayer."***

SAY: Now I will pray for each of you.

PRAY: Dear God, thank you for all of my friends here today. I pray that each of them will feel you near them this week. (Say each child's name.) In Jesus' name I pray, Amen.

Extended Discussion Questions

Use these questions to extend the activity for older children, youth, and adults:

ASK: Why do we pray for one another?

ASK: How does it feel to know that someone is praying for you?

ASK: How does it feel when what you prayed for is what happens? What about when it isn't?

Holy Moments at Home: Prayer

Dear Parents and Caregivers,

Think about the last time you had a conversation with a friend. What did the conversation look and sound like? What did the two of you talk about? How did it make you feel?

Think about the last time you prayed. What did the prayer look and sound like? What did you and God talk about? How did it make you feel?

Prayer is like having a conversation with God. There are two main parts of conversation, talking and listening. The same is true about prayer. We focus on the talking part. It can be hard to understand the listening part. What does it mean to listen when we pray? How do we listen to God?

Sometimes when we pray, we are asking God to help us or someone else. We know that God hears our prayers. What does it look, feel, and sound like when God answers?

Prayer Space

Prayer is a conversation with God that can happen anywhere. Sometimes it helps us to begin that conversation when we have a special place to pray.

- Work together to create a prayer space in your home.

- Check out https://www. pinterest.com/DeepBlueKids/ spiritual-practices/ for ideas.

Practice Conversation

- Sit down for a meal together.

- Have a conversation, being sure each family member gets an opportunity to speak and an opportunity to listen.

ASK: Is it easy or hard to be sure everyone speaks and listens?

Siren Prayers

At home or while out and about, say a prayer when you hear an emergency vehicle siren.

- Pray for the person who is having an emergency and for the emergency workers.

Prayer Board

Create a dry-erase board, chalk board, or journal where each member of the family can record the names of people or situations that he or she would like everyone to pray about.

- Take a few moments each week to pray for the names that have been recorded.

Be happy in your hope, stand your ground when you're in trouble, and devote yourselves to prayer. (Romans 12:12)

Recommended Resources for the Whole Family

When I Pray for You, Matthew Paul Turner (Picture Book - ages 3+)

Everyone Prays: Celebrating Faith Around the World, Alexis York Lumbard (Picture Book - ages 4+, Interfaith)

Journey to the Heart: Centering Prayer for Children, Frank X. Jelenek (Picture Book - ages 3+)

Praying with My Fingers: An Easy Way to Talk with God, inspired by Pope Francis (Board Book - ages 3-5)

Does God Hear My Prayer? August Gold (Picture Book - ages 4+)

This is What I Pray Today: Divine Hours Prayers for Children, Phyllis Tickle (Prayer Book - ages 3+)

Confession and Pardon

Preparing to Lead: "I'm Sorry"

As you prepare to lead this Holy Moment Activity, take some time to think about the following questions:

• How does it feel to participate in corporate confession in worship? Is this a part of the worship service that you are comfortable with, uncomfortable with, or indifferent to?

• How does it feel to know that you are forgiven? How does it feel to know that you can forgive others?

• Why is it important to say you are sorry?

Holy Moment Activity

SAY: A mistake is when we do the wrong thing. Sometimes we make mistakes without realizing. Sometimes our mistakes are because we made a bad choice. Even when we do our best to listen to God and do the things we know that we should, we still make mistakes. I make lots of mistakes.

ASK: Do you ever make mistakes? What do you do when you realize you have made a mistake?

SAY: When we come together for worship, one of the things we do is tell God about the mistakes we have made and ask for forgiveness. God already knows our mistakes, but telling God we are sorry helps us to ask for forgiveness. God always forgives when we ask.

SAY: Let's tell God about our mistakes together, and ask God to forgive us.

PRAY: Dear God, we have made lots of mistakes. We are sorry for the times when we have not listened. Please forgive us. Amen.

SAY: God promises that if we tell God our mistakes and say we are sorry, we will be forgiven. God loves you, and you are forgiven! Say that with me. **"God loves you, and you are forgiven!"**

Holy Moment Activity

Sing together, "Forgiveness" (p. 23).

Extended Discussion Questions

Use these questions to extend the activity for older children, youth, and adults:

ASK: If God knows everything, why is it important that we tell God what we have done wrong and ask for forgiveness?

ASK: Why do we say a confession together? Did we all make the same mistakes?

Passing the Peace

Preparing to Lead: "Peace Be with You"

What is "Passing the Peace," and why do we do it? In some churches, the time in the worship service labeled "Passing the Peace" is simply a time of greeting. It is placed at the beginning of the worship service and is used as a way for us to welcome one another into a space of peace. Another way that churches use the ritual is by placing it after the Confession and Pardon. Once the congregation has confessed their sins together and received and given pardon, they pass the peace of Christ to one another. It is part of an act of repentance and offer of forgiveness.

How does your congregation participate in Passing the Peace?

Holy Moment Activity

SAY: Many churches have a time during worship called Passing the Peace. We pass the peace to show that we love one another, forgive one another, and want to worship with one another. We pass the peace to show that we all are part of Jesus' family. No one is left out. Let's pass the peace together.

• Invite the children to stand in a circle and to hold hands.

• Turn to the child closest to you and say, "Peace be with you." Encourage the child to respond, "And also with you," then turn to the next child and say, "Peace be with you."

• Encourage them to continue passing the peace around the circle.

Holy Moment Activity

Supplies: crayons or markers, paper

• Write, or help a child write, "Peace be with you" on a sheet of paper.

• Invite the child to draw and color images that make him or her feel peaceful.

• Encourage the child to give their drawing to someone as a gift of peace.

Extended Discussion Questions

Use these questions to extend the activity for older children, youth, and adults:

ASK: What does peace feel like?

ASK: How do you share peace?

Holy Moments at Home: Confession, Pardon, and Passing the Peace

Dear Parents and Caregivers,

When we come together to worship, we bring all of who we are with us. We bring our happiness and love. We bring our hurts and sadness.

God wants us to be in healthy relationship with God, with one another, and with ourselves. Confessing the ways we have caused harm, forgiving and asking for forgiveness, and wishing one another peace, helps us to keep those relationships strong.

Recommended Resources for the Whole Family

Peace, Baby! Linda Ashman (Picture Book - ages 3+)

The First Strawberries: A Cherokee Story, retold by Joseph Bruchac (Picture Book - ages 4+)

Sorry! Trudy Ludwig (Picture Book - ages 6+)

The Peace Book, Todd Parr (Picture Book - ages 3+)

Confession of Sins (Chuck Knows Church Video - ages 10+) https://chuckknowschurch.com/archive/106confession-sins

Passing of the Peace (Chuck Knows Church Video - appropriate for all ages) https://chuckknowschurch.com/archive/69passing-peace

Before God and One Another: United Methodists and Confession by Joe Iovino (article - older youth and adults) http://www.umc.org/what-we-believe/before-god-and-one-another-united-methodists-and-confession

Story Time

- Read the book *What Does Peace Feel Like?* by Vladimir Radunsky.

ASK: What does peace feel like to you?

ASK: What makes you feel peaceful?

Pass the Peace

Sit down for a meal together.

- Before you eat, take turns passing peace to one another by saying, "I wish you peace."

Bedtime Prayers

- Practice ending the day by taking turns saying words of confession, forgiveness, and peace to one another.

  "I am sorry for the ways I have hurt you today."

  "Thank you for your apology. I forgive you."

PRAY: Dear God, thank you for forgiveness. Please help us to live in peace. Amen.

Balloon Prayers

SAY: Sometimes when we do things we know that we should not do or when we hurt someone, we feel sad and ashamed. Praying helps us to heal and forgive ourselves.

- Say in your heart or out loud what you would like to ask God and yourself forgiveness for.

- Blow up a balloon, imagining that your sadness and guilt are going into the balloon with the air.

- Let the air-filled balloon go.

- Imagine your mistakes and hurt floating away.

PRAY: Dear God, thank you for forgiving me. Thank you for helping me forgive myself. Amen.

But if we confess our sins, he is faithful and just to forgive us our sins and cleanse us from everything we've done wrong. (1 John 1:9)

Offering and Doxology

Preparing to Lead: Giving

When we come together for worship we often collect an offering of money. Sometimes we talk about it as our tithes and offerings. Giving a "tithe" means giving one tenth of what we have. Tithing comes from the biblical law of the Old Testament. We give our offerings to God through the church because God has given us so much. Our offerings allow us to share with others through missions. They also support salaries for pastors and other church staff, worship expenses, and the costs of keeping the church building in great shape.

As you prepare to lead this Holy Moment Activity, think about the ways you and others give to the church. Do you know what your church does with your tithes and offerings? If not, ask your pastor or a leader who works with the church's finances to share that information with you.

Holy Moment Activity

Supplies: toy money, offering plates

SAY: One of the things that we do at our church when we come together to worship is to give an offering, or money, to the church. Some families give money to the church by placing coins and paper money in the offering plate in worship. Some families write checks to place in the offering plate or send in the mail to the church. Some families give by sending money online.

ASK: How does your family give to the church? Have you ever helped your family give?

- Walk the children through what the giving and receiving of the offering looks, sounds, and feels like in your church.

- Using toy money and offering plates, encourage the children to pretend to be ushers, congregation members, and pastors.

SAY: When the ushers are finished collecting the offering, we sing a song of praise called a doxology. Let's sing a doxology together.

- Sing "Doxology," found in the column on the left.

Extended Discussion Question

Use this question to extend the activity for older children, youth, and adults:

ASK: Why do you think we sing a doxology, or a song of praise, after the offering is collected?

"Doxology" (Words: Public Domain, Tune: The United Methodist Hymnal #95)
Though one version of the Doxology is included here, you are encouraged to use the version that is commonly sung in your congregation.

Praise God, from whom all blessings flow;

praise him, all creatures here below;

praise him, above ye heavenly host;

praise Father, Son, and Holy Ghost.

Amen.

Holy Moments at Home: Offering and Doxology

Dear Parents and Caregivers,

One of the things that we do at our church when we come together to worship is to give an offering, or money, to the church. Some families give money to the church by placing coins and paper money in the offering plate in worship. Some families write checks to place in the offering plate or send in the mail to the church. Some families give by sending money online.

How does your family give to the church? How do you decide how much to give? How might you involve your children in the process?

Do you know what your church does with your tithes and offerings? Ask your pastor or a leader who works with the church's finances to share that information with your family.

Give, Save, Spend

Create three banks by using small boxes or envelopes. Label the banks *Give*, *Save*, and *Spend*.

- Work together to choose a place to support with your family's gifts of money. Write the name of the place on the *Give* bank.

- Work together to choose a goal that you would like to reach with money your family saves. It could be something like a special trip or meal. Write the goal on the *Save* bank.

- Work together to decide what the money in the *Spend* bank can be spent on and write it on the bank. You may want to choose something that you spend money on often but is a luxury.

- Once a week, give yourselves a small cash allowance as a family. Decide together how much of that allowance goes in each bank. Spend, save, and give the money accordingly.

Bedtime Prayers

Wonder together about people in your community who do not have what they need.

- How can God use your church to help? How can God use your family and your offering at church to help?

- Pray for these people and for God's guidance as a part of your bedtime prayers.

Don't forget to do good and to share what you have because God is pleased with these kinds of sacrifices. (Hebrews 13:16)

Recommended Resources for the Whole Family

Miss Fannie's Hat, Jan Karon (Picture Book - ages 3+)

In God's Hands, Rabbi Lawrence Kushner (Picture Book - ages 6+, a traditional Jewish tale)

The Giving Box: Create a Tradition of Giving with Your Children, Fred Rogers (Activity Book - all ages)

What is Given from the Heart, Patricia McKissack (Picture Book - ages 4+)

Treasure, Jacob Armstrong (Book and Study - adults)

Enough: Discovering Joy Through Simplicity and Generosity, Adam Hamilton (Book and Study - adults)

Treasures of the Transformed LIfe: Satisfy Your Soul's Thirst for More, John Ed Mathison (Book and Study - adults)

Affirmation of Faith

Preparing to Lead: We Believe

Often in worship we affirm our faith together as a response to God's Word. Sometimes we do that through saying a list of our beliefs. This list we say together is sometimes called a creed or affirmation of faith. The most common creeds or affirmations of faith used in worship are *The Apostles' Creed* and *The Nicene Creed*. Other statements used are *A Statement of Faith of the United Church of Canada*, *A Modern Affirmation*, or the *Affirmation from Romans 8:25, 37-39*.

Generally young children are not ready to study or memorize a creed or affirmation of faith. This is because most include statements and words that children are not yet able to comprehend. What they can understand and appreciate is that when the church worships together, we say what we believe. It reminds us of who we are and who God is.

Holy Moment Activity

Supplies: markers, sheets of poster paper (2)

• Place poster paper on a table or tape to a wall. Write "We believe" across the top of each one.

• Write the words *dogs* on one paper and *school* on the other.

SAY: In church we sometimes say together the things that we believe about God, Jesus, the Holy Spirit, and humans. We call that saying an Affirmation of Faith or Creed. Sometimes we all agree about what we believe, and sometimes we don't. Saying what we believe when we worship together reminds us of who we are and who God is.

Let's practice sharing what we believe with one another. We are going to share what we believe about dogs and school. It's OK if someone says they believe something that you aren't sure about or disagree with.

• Invite the children to help you list what they believe about dogs and school. Record on the poster what they say.

• Be sure each child has an opportunity to respond. If a child does not wish to share, honor that and do not force him or her to do so.

ASK: How did you decide what you believe about dogs? school?

ASK: Was sharing what you believe easy or hard? Why?

ASK: Did we always agree about what we believe? What did it feel like when we all agreed? What did it feel like when we didn't agree?

Holy Moments at Home: Affirmation of Faith

Dear Parents and Caregivers,

Often in worship we affirm our faith together as a response to God's Word. Sometimes we do that through saying a list of our beliefs. This list we say together is sometimes called a creed or affirmation of faith. The most common creeds or affirmations of faith used in worship are *The Apostles' Creed* and *The Nicene Creed*. Other statements are also used: *A Statement of Faith of the United Church of Canada*, *A Modern Affirmation*, or the *Affirmation from Romans 8:25, 37-39*.

Generally, young children are not ready to study or memorize an entire creed or affirmation of faith. This is because most include statements and words that children are not yet able to comprehend. What they can understand and appreciate is that when the church worships together, we say what we believe. It reminds us of who we are and who God is.

Memorize a Statement of Faith

- Work together to memorize all or a portion of "A Statement of Faith of the United Church of Canada." (The United Methodist Hymnal #883 or https://tinyurl.com/statementfaith)

ASK: How does it feel to know you are not alone?

ASK: What does it mean to say, "We live in God's world"?

ASK: What are the things listed in the statement of faith that God calls us to do?

ASK: Why do we remind ourselves what we believe by saying a statement of faith like this one?

Priorities and Values

SAY: When we say what we believe in church, we share what is important to us, or our priorities and values.

ASK: What do we believe?

ASK: What do we value?

ASK: What beliefs and values are most important to our family?

Write on a poster board, "In our family, we believe..."

- Work together to complete the sentence and record your thoughts in a list.
- Display your list somewhere in your home where it will be a reminder of your family's beliefs, values, and priorities.

So the churches were strengthened in the faith and every day their numbers flourished. (Acts 16:5)

Recommended Resources for the Whole Family

Faith, Maya Ajmera, Magda Nakassis, Cynthia Pon (Picture Book - ages 7+, interfaith)

Affirmation of Faith (Chuck Knows Church Video - appropriate for all ages but most interesting for ages 5+) https://chuckknowschurch.com/archive/34affirmation-faith

Top 10 United Methodist Beliefs, Don Adams (Book - adults)

What is the Apostles' Creed? Marcia Stoner (Pack of 5 Booklets - youth)

Creed: What Christians Believe and Why, Adam Hamilton (Book and Study - adults)

Baptism and Baptism Remembrance

Preparing to Lead: Touch the Water

Baptism is practiced differently across Christian traditions. In some churches, children are baptized as infants under the belief that as children of God, they are provided grace before they are even aware of such grace. In some churches, children are baptized only when they are able to make the decision for themselves to be followers of Jesus. This Holy Moment Activity and Holy Moments at Home sheet are written in a way that honors and embraces the practice of infant baptism. The children in your group may or may not have been baptized as infants. If your church does not practice infant baptism, adjust the words written in italics to fit your context. For more information on United Methodists beliefs about baptism, visit www.umc.org/what-we-believe/baptism, or check out *Touch the Water, Taste the Bread* by Daphna Flegal.

Holy Moment Activity

Supplies: fragrant lip-balm stick

SAY: Jesus was baptized in the Jordan River by his cousin, John. When Jesus came up out of the water, God said, "This is my Son whom I dearly love; I find happiness in him" (Matthew 3:17). We celebrate baptism in our church too. *In our church, we baptize people when they are babies, kids, or grown-ups. You can get baptized at any age.* The pastor will place water on the person's head (or dunk them under water in a pool) and say, "I baptize you in the name of the Father, the Son, and the Holy Spirit." *When a baby is baptized, the baby's parents and church family tell the baby and God that they will help the child learn and grow in faith. Through them and through the water, God tells the baby, "You are a child of God. I love you and find happiness in you." If you were baptized as a baby, you do not need to be baptized again. Baptism is something that only happens once.* Sometimes we use water to help us remember our baptisms. Today we will use a special blessing to help us remember that God says, "You are a child of God. I love you and find happiness in you." When it is your turn, place your hand on mine. I will rub this fragrant lip balm on your hand and speak a blessing over you.

• Invite each child, one at a time, to place their hand on yours.

• With a fragrant lip balm, draw a cross on the top of the child's hand.

• Bless the child by saying, "You are a child of God. God loves you and finds happiness in you."

• Continue until each child has received a blessing.

Holy Moment Activity

Supplies: watercolor paints, paintbrushes, cups of water

• Photocopy "Child of God" (p. 47), one for each child.

• Give each child a copy of "Child of God."

• Invite the children to paint their pictures using watercolor paint.

Holy Moments at Home: Baptism and Baptism Remembrance

Dear Parents and Caregivers,

Jesus was baptized in the Jordan River by his cousin, John. When Jesus came up out of the water, God said, "This is my Son whom I dearly love; I find happiness in him" (Matthew 3:17). We celebrate baptism in our church too. In our church, we baptize people when they are babies, kids, or grown-ups. The pastor will place water on the person's head and say, "I baptize you in the name of the Father, the Son, and the Holy Spirit." When a baby is baptized, the baby's parents and church family tell the baby and God that they will help the child learn and grow in faith. Through them and through the water, God tells the baby, "You are a child of God. I love you and find happiness in you." Sometimes we use water to help us remember our baptisms. In remembering our baptisms, we remember that God says to us, "You are a child of God. I love you and find happiness in you."

Baptism Gift

- Purchase 1.5 yards of soft fleece fabric.

- Spread the fabric on a table or on floor and cut a 1-inch square of fabric from each corner.

- Carefully cut into the fabric at 1-inch intervals to create fringe along each edge of the fabric to create a beautiful fringed blanket.

- Give the blanket to someone who has just been baptized to remind them that their church family loves them.

Water Play

- Visit a pool, lake, or ocean.

- Touch the water. If it is warm enough, go for a swim.

- If no outdoor water source is available, take turns having a warm bath.

THINK: Why does God use water to remind us we are a part of God's family?

Baptism Brownies

- Record on a calendar the date of each family member's baptism.

- On the anniversary of each baptism, bake and eat brownies to celebrate.

Family Baptisms

- Look through photographs from your family's baptisms. If you do not have any, look for images of baptisms online.

- Wonder together about what each person pictured was thinking and feeling.

There is one Lord, one faith, one baptism, and one God and Father of all, who is over all, through all, and in all. (Ephesians 4:5-6)

Recommended Resources for the Whole Family

Welcome Child of God, Anne Ylvisaker (Picture Book - ages 3+)

Come, Touch the Water: A Storybook about Jesus' Baptism, Daphna Flegal (Picture Book - ages 4-8)

Water, Come Down! The Day You Were Baptized, Walter Wangerin Jr. (Picture Book - ages 4-8)

What Is Baptism? Learning About Baptism in the United Methodist Church, G.L. Reed (Pack of 5 Booklets - youth)

Baptism (Chuck Knows Church Video - appropriate for all ages but most interesting for ages 5+) https://chuckknowschurch.com/archive/47baptism

By Water and the Spirit (PDF Book - adult) https://www.umcdiscipleship.org/resources/by-water-and-the-spirit-full-text

Confirmation and Church Membership

Preparing to Lead: We Belong Together

In traditions that baptize infants and young children, when those children get older they will be invited to go through a process called Confirmation. Unlike baptism, confirmation only happens once, but can be celebrated multiple times. Through classes and a service of commitment and celebration in worship, confirmands (people being confirmed) will decide whether they are ready to accept the commitments to faith that were made for them at their baptisms. They also make a commitment to their local community of faith and become full members of the church.

Sometimes people also join a new local congregation because they moved away from their old church or because they have found a community that is a better fit.

Confirmands and others joining the church say the same statements of faith and promise the same things to the church community. They promise to support the church with their "prayers, presence, gifts, service, and witness." The rest of the church also makes a commitment to the confirmands and new members to walk with them and support them.

Holy Moment Activity

Supplies: card stock, crayons or markers

SAY: Our church is a family. We all belong together. When someone joins our church, they say they will come to be with us, share what they have, serve others with us, and share the love of Christ with us. At baptism, the church makes the commitment to help you grow in faith, and your parents promise to help you learn more about Jesus and the church. When you are old enough to make the decision for yourself to join the church, you might go through a process called confirmation. Let's make cards to welcome our older friends who are officially joining our church family as new members or through confirmation.

- Distribute card stock.

- Direct the children to fold the card stock in half to create a card.

- Help the child write "Welcome" on the front of the card and "I'm glad you are a part of my church family" on the inside.

- Encourage the children to color and decorate the cards.

- Collect the cards and give them to the church office to mail to new members, or ask for a list of new members so you may send the cards yourself.

This Holy Moment Activity is based upon the liturgy of the United Methodist Church. The order of worship for welcoming new members and for confirmation, including membership vows, can be found in *The United Methodist Book of Worship* (pp. 86-94). For more information, see *Our Membership Vows in the United Methodist Church* by Mark W. Stamm, available online at https://www.umcdiscipleship.org/resources/our-membership-vows-in-the-united-methodist-church.

Holy Moments at Home: Confirmation and Church Membership

Dear Parents and Caregivers,

In traditions that baptize infants and young children, when those children become older, they will be invited to go through a process called confirmation. Through classes and a service of commitment and celebration in worship, confirmands (people being confirmed) will decide if they are ready to accept the commitments to faith that were made for them at their baptisms. They also make a commitment to their local community of faith and become full members of the church.

Confirmands and others joining the church say the same statements of faith and promise the same things to the church community. They promise to support the church with their "prayers, presence, gifts, service, and witness." The rest of the church also makes a commitment to the confirmands and new members to walk with them and support them.

Presence

- Attend worship together as a family.

- After worship, greet someone you do not know or have not seen in a while. Let them know that you are glad you worshiped with them.

I See God's Family

ASK: What does the family of God look like?

- Spend some time sitting together on a park bench or at a table in a shopping center.

- Watch people as they pass by.

- Remind one another that each person you see is a part of the family of God.

What is Confirmation?

- Ask your pastor or children's minister to help you identify someone who was recently confirmed and would be willing to help your family learn more.

- Spend some time with the confirmation student, asking any questions you have about the process.

Pray for Your Church

- Look through a church pictorial directory, church photo album, or church website. Choose three or four images.

- Pray together for the members of God's family who are in each picture.

In the same way, though there are many of us, we are one body in Christ, and individually we belong to each other. (Romans 12:5)

Recommended Resources for the Whole Family

Confirmation and Confirmation 2 (Chuck Knows Church Video - appropriate for all ages but most interesting for ages 10+) https://chuckknowschurch.com/archive/43confirmation and https://chuckknowschurch.com/archive/76confirmation-part-2

Beyond Baptism: What Confirmation Means to United Methodists by Joe Iovino (Article - youth and adults)http://www.umc.org/what-we-believe/beyond-baptism-what-confirmation-means-to-united-methodists

I Promise, David McPhail (Picture Book - ages 3+)

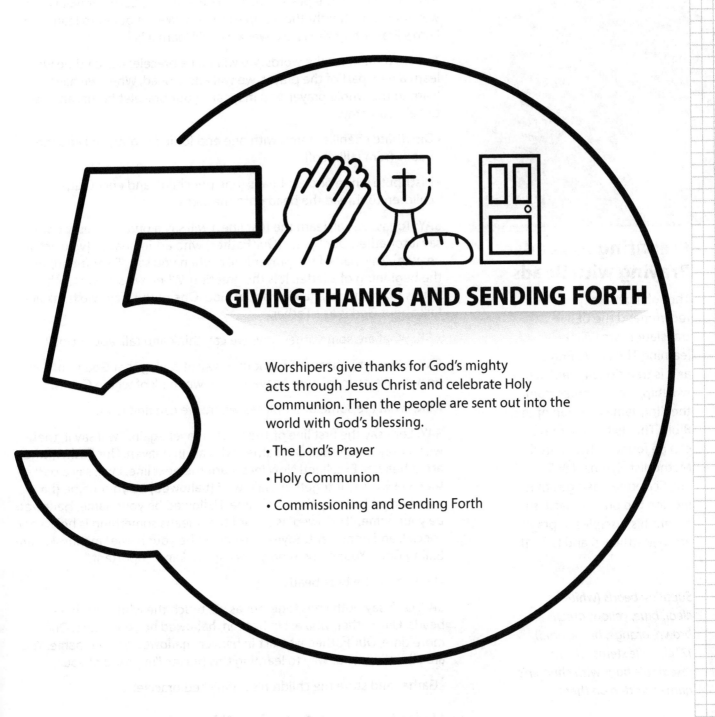

5

GIVING THANKS AND SENDING FORTH

Worshipers give thanks for God's mighty acts through Jesus Christ and celebrate Holy Communion. Then the people are sent out into the world with God's blessing.

- The Lord's Prayer

- Holy Communion

- Commissioning and Sending Forth

The Lord's Prayer

Holy Moment Activity: Week 1

SAY: When we worship at church, we often say a special prayer together. We call the prayer The Lord's Prayer. The Lord's Prayer is the way that Jesus taught the disciples to pray. We are going to learn The Lord's Prayer together. Each week we will learn a line.

To help remember the words, we will make bracelets. Each time we learn a new part of the prayer, we will add a bead. When we have learned the whole prayer, you may take your bracelet home, and use it to help you pray.

- Distribute chenille stems, with one end folded slightly to keep the beads from falling off.
- Distribute white or clear beads (one per child), and encourage children to thread the bead onto the stem.

SAY: Today we will learn the first line. I will say a phrase, then we will say it together. Our Father **(Our Father)** who art in heaven **(who art in heaven)**. This part of the prayer is like when you say, "Dear friend," at the beginning of a letter. It is the greeting. When we say "Our Father" in this prayer, we are talking about God. One of the ways we think and talk about God is as a Father.

ASK: What are some other ways we can think and talk about God?

SAY: "Who art in heaven," is another way of saying that God is in heaven. We often picture heaven when we think of where God is.

ASK: What are some other places where we can find God?

SAY: Let's say the first line of The Lord's Prayer again. I will say it, then we will say it together. Our Father, who art in heaven, **Our Father, who art in heaven.** Excellent! Now let's learn the next line. I will say a part, then we will say it together. Hallowed **(hallowed)** be your name **(be your name.)** Let's say the whole line. Hallowed be your name. **Hallowed be your name.** "Hallowed" is a word that means something is holy, very special, and important. Saying "hallowed be your name" means you are telling God, "Your name is holy, very special and important."

- Distribute the blue beads.

SAY: Let's say both lines together as we touch the white and blue beads. **Our Father, who art in heaven, hallowed be your name.** One more time, **Our Father, who art in heaven, hallowed be your name.** You are all well on your way to learning this prayer. I'm proud of you.

- Gather and store the children's unfinished bracelets.

Holy Moment Activity: Week 2

SAY: When we worship at church, we often say a special prayer together. We call the prayer The Lord's Prayer. The Lord's Prayer is the way that Jesus taught the disciples to pray. We are learning the prayer together. To help us remember the words, we are making bracelets.

Preparing to Lead: Praying with Beads

Though I generally recommend the CEB translation, we will be learning The Lord's Prayer as it is traditionally said in worship, which comes from the King James Version of the Bible. The text of the prayer can be found in the United Methodist Hymnal #895. The Scripture passages that include the prayer that Jesus taught his disciples to pray are in Matthew 6 and Luke 11.

Supplies: beads (white or clear, blue, yellow, green, brown, orange, black, gold), 12" chenille stems, plastic resealable bags with children's names written on them

The Lord's Prayer

Each time we learn a new part of the prayer, we will add beads. When we have learned the whole prayer, you may take your bracelet home, and use it to help you pray.

• Distribute the children's unfinished bracelets.

SAY: Touch the white bead. This bead reminds us of the first line of the prayer. I will say it, then we will say it together. Our Father, who art in heaven, **Our Father, who art in heaven.** Excellent memory! Touch the blue bead. This bead reminds us of the second line of the prayer. I will say it, then we will say it together. Hallowed be your name. **Hallowed be your name.** Great work!

• Distribute the yellow beads.

SAY: Let's learn the next line. I will say a phrase, then we will say it together. Thy kingdom come **(Thy kingdom come)**, thy will be done **(thy will be done).** Let's say the whole line. Thy kingdom come, thy will be done. **Thy kingdom come, thy will be done.** When we say "Thy kingdom come, thy will be done," we are saying, "God, we want the whole world to be like heaven. We know that what you want to happen is what is best and most important."

• Distribute the green beads.

SAY: Let's learn another line today. I will say it, then we will say it together. On earth as it is in heaven **(on earth as it is in heaven).** Wonderful! This is another way to say we want earth to be like heaven.

SAY: Together let's touch each bead and say all of the lines we have learned so far. It is OK if you have a little trouble. Learning long prayers like this takes practice, and we will keep practicing together. Start by touching your white bead. (white) **Our Father, who art in heaven,** (blue) **hallowed be thy name.** (yellow) **Thy kingdom come, thy will be done** (green) **on earth as it is in heaven.**

SAY: That was really good remembering! I'm proud of you.

• You may wish to repeat the prayer a few times if the children show interest. Then gather and store the unfinished bracelets.

Holy Moment Activity: Week 3

SAY: We have been learning The Lord's Prayer together. The Lord's Prayer is the way that Jesus taught the disciples to pray. Each time we learn a new part of the prayer, we add a bead to our bracelets. When we have learned the whole prayer, you may take your bracelet home and use it when you pray.

• Distribute the children's unfinished bracelets.

SAY: We have already learned four parts of the Lord's Prayer. Let's touch each bead and say what we remember together. It is OK if you have a little trouble. Learning long prayers like this takes practice, and we will keep practicing together.

TIPS:

• After the first week, prepare chenille stems with beads for children who were not in attendance in previous weeks.

• Write names on plastic bags or insert slips of paper with each child's name on them. Store bags in a safe place between weekly activities.

• Be sure to fold down both ends of the chenille stems before storing so that the beads do not fall off.

• For younger children, you may wish to separate these activities into more than four weeks, adding only one bead each week.

The Lord's Prayer

Start by touching the white bead. (white) **Our Father, who art in heaven,** (blue) **hallowed be thy name.** (yellow) **Thy kingdom come, thy will be done** (green) **on earth as it is in heaven.**

• Distribute the brown beads.

SAY: Now we will add a brown bead, and learn the next line of the prayer. I will say it, then we will say it together. Give us this day our daily bread **(Give us this day our daily bread).** Wonderful! When we pray this line, we are saying that we trust God to give us what we need each day. Do you think we can say every part of the prayer we have learned so far?

Start by touching the white bead. (white) **Our Father, who art in heaven,** (blue) **hallowed be thy name.** (yellow) **Thy kingdom come, thy will be done** (green) **on earth as it is in heaven.** (brown) **Give us this day our daily bread.**

SAY: Each time we say the prayer, we remember the words a little more easily. You are doing a great job! Let's learn one more part.

• Distribute the orange beads.

SAY: This part of the prayer includes an interesting word: *trespass*. In The Lord's Prayer, "trespass" means doing something wrong or unkind to another person. When we trespass against someone, we ask for forgiveness. This part of the prayer is longer, so we will learn it in three sections. I will say a section, then we will say it together. Forgive us our trespasses, **(Forgive us our trespasses)** as we forgive those **(as we forgive those)** who trespass against us **(who trespass against us.)** Great! Now let's say the entire line. Forgive us our trespasses, as we forgive those who trespass against us. **(Forgive us our trespasses, as we forgive those who trespass against us.)** Wonderful! When we pray this line, we ask God to forgive us when we do things that are wrong or unkind. We also remind ourselves to be forgiving to others who do something wrong or unkind to us.

Do you think we can say all of the prayer that we have learned so far? I think we can. Start by touching your white bead. (white) **Our Father, who art in heaven,** (blue) **hallowed be thy name.** (yellow) **Thy kingdom come, thy will be done** (green) **on earth as it is in heaven.** (brown) **Give us this day our daily bread.** (orange) **And forgive us our trespasses, as we forgive those who trespass against us.** You have almost learned the entire prayer. Each time we say the prayer, we will remember the words a little more easily. You are doing a great job!

• You may wish to repeat the prayer a few times if the children show interest. Then gather and store the children's unfinished bracelets.

Holy Moment Activity: Week 4

SAY: We have been learning The Lord's Prayer together. The Lord's Prayer is the way that Jesus taught the disciples to pray. We are making bracelets to help us remember the words. Today we will add the last two beads. Then you may take your bracelet home, and use it to help you remember as you pray.

TIPS:

• After the first week, prepare chenille stems with beads for children who were not in attendance in previous weeks.

• Write names on plastic bags or insert slips of paper with each child's name on them. Store bags in a safe place between weekly activities.

• Be sure to fold down both ends of the chenille stems before storing so that the beads do not fall off.

• For younger children, you may wish to separate these activities into more than four weeks, adding only one bead each week.

The Lord's Prayer

- Distribute the children's unfinished bracelets.

SAY: Let's touch each bead and say what we have learned so far. It is OK if you have a little bit of trouble. Learning long prayers like this takes practice, and we will keep practicing together. Start by touching the white bead. (white) **Our Father, who art in heaven,** (blue) **hallowed be thy name.** (yellow) **Thy kingdom come, thy will be done** (green) **on earth as it is in heaven.** (brown) **Give us this day our daily bread.** (orange) **Forgive us our trespasses, as we forgive those who trespass against us.**

- Distribute the black beads.

SAY: Ready to learn the next part? I will say a section, then we will say it together. Lead us not into temptation, **(Lead us not into temptation,)** but deliver us from evil **(but deliver us from evil).** Awesome! Let's say the two sections at once. Lead us not into temptation, but deliver us from evil. **Lead us not into temptation, but deliver us from evil.** Wonderful! When we pray this line, we ask God to help us stay away from things that are not good for us. We ask God to help us stay away from things that tempt us to do hurtful things.

Do you think we can say all of the prayer that we have learned so far? I think we can. Touch the white bead. (white) **Our Father, who art in heaven,** (blue) **hallowed be thy name.** (yellow) **Thy kingdom come, thy will be done** (green) **on earth as it is in heaven.** (brown) **Give us this day our daily bread.** (orange) **And forgive us our trespasses, as we forgive those who trespass against us.** (black) **Lead us not into temptation, but deliver us from evil.** Almost there! You are doing a great job!

- Distribute the gold beads.

SAY: Now we will learn the last part of the prayer. There are three things that we say belong to God. Repeat after me: kingdom **(kingdom)**, power **(power)**, glory **(glory)**. In the prayer, we say it like this, "For thine is the kingdom, and the power, and the glory, forever." Say that with me. **For thine is the kingdom, and the power, and the glory, forever.** And we end the prayer with a big, "Amen!" Say the whole line with me. **For thine is the kingdom, and the power, and the glory, forever. Amen!**

You have learned the whole prayer! Let's say the whole prayer together. Touch the white bead. (white) **Our Father, who art in heaven,** (blue) **hallowed be thy name.** (yellow) **Thy kingdom come, thy will be done** (green) **on earth as it is in heaven.** (brown) **Give us this day our daily bread.** (orange) **And forgive us our trespasses, as we forgive those who trespass against us.** (black) **And lead us not into temptation, but deliver us from evil.** (gold) **For thine is the kingdom, and the power, and the glory, forever. Amen!**

SAY: I am proud of you for working so hard to learn this prayer! Take your bracelet home with you, and use it to help you remember. The more you practice the prayer, the easier it will be to remember.

- Show the children how to join the stem ends to make the bracelets, then put the bracelets on their wrists.

TIPS:

- After the first week, prepare chenille stems with beads for children who were not in attendance in previous weeks.

- Write names on plastic bags or insert slips of paper with each child's name on them. Store bags in a safe place between weekly activities.

- Be sure to fold down both ends of the chenille stems before storing so that the beads do not fall off.

- For younger children, you may wish to separate these activities into more than four weeks, adding only one bead each week.

Holy Communion

Preparing to Lead

Use this Holy Moment as a very basic guide for talking about how your church celebrates Holy Communion. Some pieces may need to be adjusted for your particular context. The Holy Moment Activity includes sharing a snack together. If your context and tradition allows, feel free to modify this to a full celebration of communion.

Holy Moment Activity

Supplies: crackers (bite-sized), cups (small), water

SAY: In our church we celebrate a special meal together called Holy Communion. Communion isn't a meal where everyone sits down at a table and has meat, bread, vegetables, and fruit. Communion is a small taste of bread and grape juice that reminds us that we are all invited to Jesus' table. The words of communion remind us of the meal Jesus celebrated with his disciples before he went to the cross. When you are with your family in worship, and when you and your family decide you are ready, you will get to celebrate communion, too.

ASK: Have you ever taken communion in worship? What was it like?

Eating together is special. Your family eats together, Jesus ate with his disciples, and we eat together, too. Though we are not celebrating Holy Communion today, we will share a special snack and blessing.

• Gather the children in a circle or line and give each child a cup of crackers and a cup of water.

• Bless them by saying "God loves you. You are a child of God."

Holy Moment Activity

Supplies: crayons

• Photocopy "Mealtime Blessings" (p. 57), one for each child.

• Give each child a copy of "Mealtime Blessings."

• Invite the children to fold the paper into a book and color the images.

• Read or sing the blessings together.

NOTE: There are many words for Holy Communion, such as Eucharist and the Lord's Supper. Feel free to use the language of your tradition.

Extended Discussion Questions

Use these questions to extend the activity for older children, youth, and adults:

ASK: Why do we take Holy Communion? Why did Jesus tell his disciples to remember him in this way?

• Read through your church's communion liturgy together. What questions do you have? Who might you ask to help you answer them?

Mealtime Blessings

Lord, we thank You,
Lord, we thank You,

For our food,
For our food,

And our many blessings,
and our many blessings.

Amen.
Amen.

(Tune: Frere Jacques,
Source: Public domain)

God is great!
God is good!
Let us thank
GOD
For our food.
Amen.

(Source: Public domain)

Thank you
for the food we eat,
Thank you
for the world so sweet,
Thank you
for the birds that sing,
Thank you
God for everything
Amen.

(Source: Public domain)

Holy Moments at Home: Holy Communion

Dear Parents and Caregivers,

In our church we celebrate a special meal together called Holy Communion. Communion isn't a meal where everyone sits down at a table and has meat, bread, vegetables, and fruit. It is a small taste of bread and grape juice that reminds us that we are all invited to Jesus' table. The words of communion remind us of the meal Jesus celebrated with his disciples before he went to the cross.

Eating together is something that is very special. Your family eats together, you eat with your friends, and Jesus ate with his disciples. We eat together, too.

There is no right or wrong time for a child to begin taking communion at church. Your child may begin celebrating Holy Communion when he or she and your family decides they are ready. For guidance on your local church tradition, see your pastor or children's minister.

Baking Unleavened Bread

- Mix the following ingredients in a large bowl: all-purpose flour (1 cup), vegetable oil (1/3 cup), salt (1/8 teaspoon).
- Add water (1/3 cup) and mix until the dough is soft.
- Line a baking sheet with parchment paper.
- Divide the dough into six parts.
- Roll each part into a ball. Then flatten.
- Place the flattened dough on the baking sheet.
- Bake at 425 degrees for 8 to 10 minutes.
- Enjoy eating the bread together as a snack.

A Family Meal

- As a family, plan to have a special meal together.
- Decide which family member will be in charge of each aspect of the meal according to what they do well. Who will set the table? cook? pour the drinks?
- Decide when your special meal will be, and put the date on the calendar.
- Share your special meal together.

Serve and Share

- Serve as a family at a local food bank, community garden, or soup kitchen. If your church isn't already involved with an organization, find one at www.feedingamerica.org or www.volunteermatch.org.

"This is my body, which is given for you. Do this in remembrance of me." (Luke 22:19b)

Recommended Resources for the Whole Family

Come, Taste the Bread: A Storybook About the Lord's Supper, Daphna Flegal (Picture Book - ages 4-8)

Bread Comes to Life: A Garden of Wheat and a Loaf to Eat, George Levenson (Picture Book - ages 3+)

Communion (Chuck Knows Church Video - appropriate for all ages but most interesting for ages 10+) https://chuckknowschurch.com/archive/24communion

The Bread and Cup (Chuck Knows Church Video - appropriate for all ages but most interesting for ages 10+) https://chuckknowschurch.com/archive/27the-bread-and-cup

What Is Communion? Learning About Communion in the United Methodist Church, G.L. Reed (Pack of 5 Booklets - youth)

Commissioning and Sending Forth

Preparing to Lead: Go Now In Peace

You entered into worship to pray, sing, and listen. Now it is time to go back out into the world to pray, sing, and listen there. We, too, are called to go out and serve others and to share God's love through Jesus Christ. We are called to go to share the love that can change the world! All worship services will end with some type of sung or spoken benediction.

Sometimes your worship service also may include a time of *commissioning*. Comissioning is a special call to go serve for a specific purpose. Generally commissioning happens when a group or person is going on a mission trip or beginning a new ministry.

Holy Moment Activity

SAY: The benediction is a blessing the pastor or other leader gives at the very end of worship time to everyone worshiping together. Sometimes a benediction is said from the back of the worship space. Sometimes the pastor raises his or her hands. Sometimes the benediction is said by all of the worshipers together. Sometimes the worshipers hold hands and look at one another's faces as the benediction is spoken. No matter where or how it is said, a benediction is a blessing that we wish for one another.

ASK: Do we have a benediction in our worship service? What does it look and sound like?

SAY: Today I would like to say a blessing benediction for you from the Bible. It comes from Numbers 6:24-26.

PRAY: "The Lord bless you and protect you. The Lord make his face shine on you and be gracious to you. The Lord lift up his face to you and grant you peace." Amen.

Holy Moments at Home: Commissioning and Sending Forth

Dear Parents and Caregivers,

Just like we have Holy Moments for entering into worship, we have Holy Moments for ending our worship time. You entered into worship to pray, sing, and listen. Now it is time to go back out into the world to pray, sing, and listen there. We, too, are called to go out and serve others and to share God's love through Jesus Christ. We are called to go to share the love that can change the world!

All worship services will end with some type of sung or spoken benediction. Usually the pastor or another leader will stand facing the worshipers, remind everyone that God is calling them to be followers of Christ in the world, and give them a blessing.

Where?

- Read a storybook together, such as *Where Are You Hiding, God?* by Elisabeth Zartl.

- Wonder together about where God is.

ASK: Does God live at church? Is God in heaven? Does God live in your heart? Is God everywhere?

May I Be Excused?

- Sit down for a meal together and discuss these questions as you eat.

ASK: How do you know when time together at a party has ended and it is time to do something different? At home? At school? At church?

ASK: How do we decide when it is time to end our dinner?

Pray Them Out

- Each day this week, take a moment to pray for one another before everyone leaves the house.

PRAY: God be with you as you go! Amen.

What Is a Blessing?

- Look up the word "blessing" in a Bible dictionary such as the *Deep Blue Kids Bible Dictionary*.

- Look up the word in a regular English dictionary.

ASK: How are the definitions the same? How are they different?

The LORD bless you and protect you. The LORD make his face shine on you and be gracious to you. The LORD lift up his face to you and grant you peace. (Numbers 6:24-26)

Recommended Resources for the Whole Family

This is the Church, Sarah Raymond Cunningham (Picture Book - ages 3+)

Come with Me, Holly M. McGhee (Picture Book - ages 3+)

Miss Maple's Seeds, Eliza Wheeler (Picture Book - ages 3+)

Where Are You Hiding, God? Elisabeth Zartl (Picture Book - ages 3+)

When Helping Hurts: How to Alleviate Poverty Without Hurting the Poor...and Yourself, Steve Corbett (Book - adults and older teens)

The Great Commission (Chuck Knows Church Video - youth and adults) https://chuckknowschurch.com/archive/83great-commission

Special Days and Seasons

- Advent
- Christmas
- Ash Wednesday
- Holy Week and Easter
- Pentecost
- All Saints' Day

Advent

Preparing to Lead: Celebrating Advent

There is a feeling in the air that wasn't there before. There is an underlying anticipation and excitement to everything we do. It's Advent!

Advent is the season of preparation for Christmas, the celebration of Jesus' birth. It is also a time when we remember and celebrate our preparation for Jesus' return. It is common practice to display an Advent wreath and light candles each week. The lit candles show us the passage of time and remind us that the light of Christ is coming into the world. Some churches use four purple candles, the color of the liturgical season. Some use four blue candles to distinguish Advent from Lent, which shares purple as a liturgical color. And some churches use three purple candles and one rose-colored candle. The rose-colored candle is lit on the third Sunday of Advent, also called Gaudete or Joy Sunday. In many churches, a white candle is added in the center of the wreath to be lit on Christmas Eve or Christmas Day.

The four weeks in Advent are commonly named Hope, Love, Joy, and Peace. During worship each week, someone will light the candle representing the current week, as well as the candles representing the previous weeks. Then the congregation prays together. As you prepare for using these Advent Holy Moment Activities, spend some time thinking about how your church celebrates Advent. What parts of the celebration have been most meaningful for you?

• Place an Advent wreath in the worship space. Place four candles in the wreath. The candles may be regular candles, or you may choose to use battery-powered candles, depending on the rules in your space.

OPTION: Photocopy the Advent Calendar (p. 65) for each child. Send the calendar home and encourage the children to color the boxes throughout the season of Advent.

Holy Moment Activity: Advent 1—Hope

SAY: Today we are beginning a special season in our church. This season helps us get ready for Christmas. Do you know what the season is called? (Advent) We celebrate Advent in a lot of different ways in our church. One way we celebrate is to light the candles on an Advent wreath. Each candle represents a week in Advent. How many candles do you see? (4) What color are they? (blue or purple and pink)

The candle we light today has a special name. We call it the Hope candle. We will light the candle and pray together. Next week we will light this candle again, and also light the next candle. Let's pray together as we light the Hope candle.

(Advent prayers adapted from the United Methodist Book of Worship, pages 262-263).

Advent

PRAY: O God, we light this candle to remind us that Jesus is our hope. May this light sent from God shine in the darkness. O come, O come, Emmanuel. Amen.

Holy Moment Activity: Advent 2—Love

SAY: We celebrate the season of Advent. Advent is a time of waiting for Jesus to be born.

We celebrate Advent in a lot of different ways in our church. One way we celebrate is to light the candles on an Advent wreath. Each candle represents a week in Advent. How many candles do you see? (4) What color are they? (blue or purple and pink)

Last week we lit the Hope candle. Today we light the Hope candle again, and also light the Love candle. Next week we will light three candles. Let's light the candles and pray together.

PRAY: O God, we light this candle to remind us that Jesus is love. May this love sent through Jesus lead us closer to God. O come, O come, Emmanuel. Amen.

(Advent prayers adapted from the United Methodist Book of Worship, pages 262-263.)

Holy Moment Activity: Advent 3—Joy

SAY: Today we celebrate the third Sunday of Advent. We celebrate Advent in a lot of different ways in our church. One way we celebrate is to light the candles on an Advent wreath. Each candle represents a week in Advent.

Do you remember the names of the first two candles we lit? Today we light them again. First we light the Hope candle. Jesus' birth gives us hope. Then we light the Love candle. Jesus' birth shows us that God loves the world. Today we light the Joy candle. Jesus brings joy to the world. Let's pray together as we light the Joy candle.

PRAY: O God, we light this candle to remind us that Jesus is our joy. May our joy shine bright like this candle. O come, O come, Emmanuel. Amen.

Holy Moment Activity: Advent 4—Peace

SAY: Today is the last Sunday in the season of Advent. We celebrate Advent in a lot of different ways in our church. One way we celebrate is to light the candles on an Advent wreath. Let's count the candles in our Advent wreath. (1,2,3,4) We have lit the Hope candle, the Love candle, and the Joy candle. Today we will light the Peace candle. Let's light the four candles as we pray.

PRAY: O God, we light this candle to remind us that Jesus is the Prince of Peace. We pray that the Holy Spirit will make us ready for the hope, love, joy, and peace of Jesus. O come, O come, Emmanuel. Amen.

Christmas

Preparing to Lead: That's All He Wrote

Luke 2:1-7 contains the entirety of Jesus' birth narrative. Matthew gives us a story of Mary and Joseph learning of Mary's miraculous pregnancy. The only thing Matthew tells us about Jesus being born is in Matthew 1:25 where we learn that Joseph, "didn't have sexual relations with her until she gave birth to a son." Then the Gospel writer skips to the visit from the magi. The Gospel of Mark jumps over Jesus' young life entirely, and begins with his baptism and early ministry. The Gospel of John gives us a wildly different beginning with beautiful imagery, but no birth story. I wonder why Luke is the only Gospel that tells us of the events of Jesus' actual birth. What do you think?

Here is what we know about Jesus' birth from those seven short verses:

When Quirinius governed Syria, Caesar Augustus said everyone must be counted and added to the census list for taxes. Joseph was required to go to David's city, Bethlehem, to be counted. Of course, Mary went, too. She had a baby while they were there. There was no room for them in the guest room. Mary wrapped Jesus and placed him in a manger.

That's it! That is all we know about Jesus' birthday. Over time tradition has given us a larger picture of that "Silent Night," and filled in some details for us to imagine what it must have been like. We usually see Mary depicted riding a donkey with Joseph beside her. While this travel plan is probable, there are other ways the couple could have traveled. We don't know for sure if Joseph and Mary were turned away from one inn, but accepted at an inn that had a stable for them to stay in. We only know that there was no room for them in a guest room, and Mary placed Jesus in a manger, which was a feeding trough for animals.

Luke could have told us so much more about Jesus' birth. I wonder why the Gospel writer only chose these few details. I wonder what Jesus and his parents shared with others about his birth story. What do you think? What did your parents share with you about your birth story? What do you share about the birth story(ies) of your child(ren)?

Holy Moment Activity

Supplies: set of unbreakable (fabric, paper, or plastic) Nativity figures, including the Holy Family, the stable and manger, and animals

• Place unbreakable Nativity figures on a table or on the floor. Invite the children to play freely with the figures.

• Use the figures to retell the story of Jesus' birth.

Advent Calendar

SUNDAY	MONDAY	TUESDAY	WEDNESDAY	THURSDAY	FRIDAY	SATURDAY
	H	O	P	E		
	L	O	V	E		
	J	O	Y			

CHRISTMAS EVE

PEACE

CHRISTMAS

Holy Moments at Home: Advent

Dear Parents and Caregivers,

Advent is the season of preparation for Christmas, the celebration of Jesus' birth. It is also a time when we remember and celebrate our preparation for Jesus' return. During this season we light an Advent wreath. The lit candles show us the passage of time and remind us that the light of Christ is coming into the world. Some churches use four purple candles, the color of the liturgical season. Some use four blue candles to distinguish Advent from Lent, which shares purple as a liturgical color. And some churches use three purple candles and one rose-colored candle. The rose-colored candle is lit on the third Sunday. In many churches, a white candle is added in the center of the wreath to be lit on Christmas Eve or Christmas Day. Do you remember using an Advent wreath when you were a child? What color were the candles?

Tour of Lights

- Grab some hot cocoa, hop in the car, and tour the neighborhood or city. Look at the holiday decorations and lights. Sing or listen to your favorite Christmas songs.

ASK: Why do people decorate for Christmas?

ASK: How does your family prepare for Jesus' birth?

Create Advent Wreath

- Create an Advent Wreath together.

- Check out https://www.pinterest.com/DeepBlueKids/adventchristmas/ for ideas and instructions.

- Light your Advent Wreath once a week, each week until Christmas.

Happy Advent!

- Visit a friend or family member that you have not seen in a while and wish them "Happy Advent."

- Or visit a local nursing or retirement home to wish the residents there a "Happy Advent" and "Merry Christmas." Be sure to call before you visit!

Jesus' Birth Story

- Light a candle. If you are using an Advent wreath, use those candles.

- Read about Jesus' birth from Luke 2:1-20.

ASK: What do you think it was like when Jesus was born?

ASK: What details do we learn from the Bible? What details have we added from tradition?

The true light that shines on all people was coming into the world. (John 1:9)

Recommended Resources for the Whole Family

Who Is Coming to Our House? Joseph Slate (Picture Book - ages 2+)

Brown Bear's Wonderful Secret, Caroline Castle (Picture Book - ages 3+)

Keep Watch with Me: An Advent Reader for Peacemakers, Claire Brown and Michael T. McRay (Devotional Book - adult)

Advent Wreath (Chuck Knows Church Video - all ages) https://chuckknowschurch.com/archive/5advent-wreath

The Advent Jesse Tree: Devotions for Children and Adults to Prepare for the Coming of the Christ Child at Christmas, Dean Lambert Smith (Devotional Book - all ages)

Holy Moments at Home: Christmas and Epiphany

Dear Parents and Caregivers,

Luke 2:1-7 contains all we really know about Jesus' birth. Here's what we know: When Quirinius governed Syria, Caesar Augustus said everyone must be counted and added to the census list for taxes. Joseph was required to go to David's city, Bethlehem, to be counted. Mary, of course, went, too. She had a baby while they were there. There was no room for them in the guest room. Mary wrapped Jesus and placed him in a manger.

That's it! That is all we know about Jesus' birth. Over time, tradition has given us a larger picture of that "Silent Night," and filled in some details for us to imagine what it must have been like. Luke could have told us so much more about Jesus' birth. What do you imagine that Jesus' parents shared with friends and family about his birth story? What did your parents share with you about your birth story? What do you share about the birth story(ies) of your child(ren)?

Bedtime Story

- Read a favorite Christmas story together at bedtime.

- Wonder together about bedtime for Jesus. Did Mary and Joseph sing lullabies to the baby Jesus or tell him bedtime stories?

Live Nativity

- Visit a live Nativity or a place where you might be able to see live sheep.

ASK: What do you think being a shepherd back then was like? Was it an easy or difficult job?

ASK: How do you imagine the shepherds felt when the angel appeared?

ASK: How do you imagine they felt when they saw Jesus for the first time?

Bless This House

- The Magi brought blessings for Jesus and his family. Bless your home as a family using this traditional blessing.

- Use chalk to write "20 + C + M + B + 00." Fill in the last two numbers with the current year.

The numbers are a symbol of the new year. The C, M, and B may stand for the traditional three names of the magi (Caspar, Melchior, and Balthazar), or they may also stand for "Christus Mansionem Benedictat," which means " May Christ Bless This House" in Latin. The + signs represent the four seasons of the year.

PRAY: God of love, bless this house and everyone who lives inside. Fill us with the light of Christ so we can reflect your love to all we meet. Amen.

"Your savior is born today in the David's city. He is Christ the Lord." (Luke 2:11)

Recommended Resources for the Whole Family

Refuge, Anne Booth and Sam Usher (Picture Book - ages 3+)

A Manger Miracle: A Christmas Activity Book, Erin R. Floyd (Picture Book (Pack of 10) - ages 3+)

Twas the Evening of Christmas, Glenys Nellist (Picture Book - ages 3+)

A Savior is Born: Rocks Tell the Story of Christmas, Patti Rokus (Picture Book - all ages)

The Story of the Three Wise Kings, Tomie dePaola (Picture Book - ages 3+)

Epiphany (Chuck Knows Church Video - all ages) https://chuckknowschurch.com/archive/59epiphany

Ash Wednesday and Lent

Preparing to Lead: Ashes, Ashes

The season of Lent is a time when we remember Jesus' life and death, and prepare to celebrate his Resurrection on Easter. Ash Wednesday, the first day of Lent, is observed by having ashes from last year's palm branches placed on your forehead in the shape of a cross. This is a sign of repentance, or saying, "I'm sorry," and it is a reminder that we are human. The person drawing the cross will usually say, "Repent, and believe in the Gospel," or "Remember that you are dust, and to dust you shall return."

On Ash Wednesday and throughout Lent we are reminded that we are living humans who one day will physically die. Death and dying can be a difficult subject for all of us to talk about. It can be especially difficult to answer kids' questions. Remember, it is OK to say, "I don't know. Let's think about it together."

Holy Moment Activity

Supplies: box, black ribbon, crayons or markers

- Photocopy "Alleluia" (p. 69) for each child.

- Give each child a copy of "Alleluia" and invite the children to color it.

SAY: During the season of Lent, we remember Jesus and prepare our hearts for his death and resurrection. We know that Jesus was killed on the cross, and it makes us very sad. But we already know the best news! Jesus rose again! Jesus is alive! Alleluia!

During the season of Lent, one tradition is to fast from, or stop from, saying the word "Alleluia." Alleluia is a joyful word. When we decide to stop saying it for a while, we are reminded that Jesus' death is not joyful. Let's observe this tradition together. We are going to put away our "Alleluias." Guess what, though? We get to bring them back out on Easter Sunday!

- Show the children the box, then invite each child to say the word "Alleluia" and place his or her paper into the box.

- Close the box, and tie the black ribbon around it to keep it closed. Place the box in a location where the children can still see it.

- Remember to open the box on Easter, or shortly thereafter. Give each child his or her papers and shout a big "Alleluia!" together.

Holy Moment Activity

Supplies: small bowl containing a mixture of olive oil and palm ashes

- For each child who wishes to participate, place the sign of the cross in ashes on the child's forehead.

- Say to each child, "Remember, you are human. You are a child of God."

Alleluia

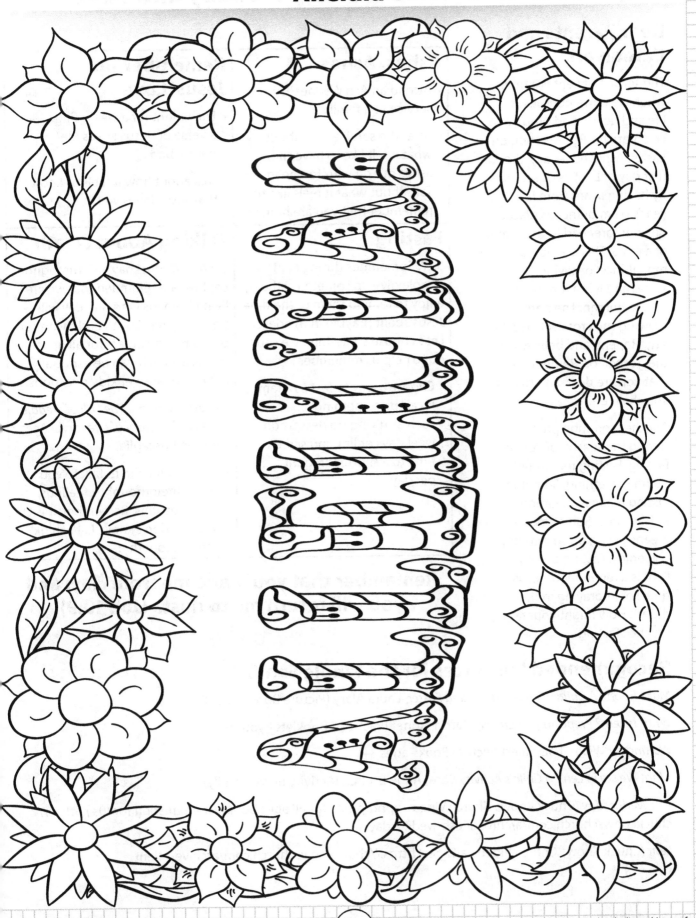

Holy Moments at Home: Ash Wednesday and Lent

Dear Parents and Caregivers,

The season of Lent is a time when we remember Jesus' life and death, and prepare to celebrate his Resurrection on Easter. Ash Wednesday, the first day of Lent, is observed by having ashes from last year's palm branches placed on your forehead in the shape of a cross. This is a sign of repentance, or saying, "I'm sorry," and it is a reminder that we are human. The person drawing the cross will usually say, "Repent, and believe in the gospel" or "Remember that you are dust, and to dust you shall return."

Another common practice during the season of Lent is fasting. Fasting means not doing something. Sometimes fasting means not eating for a short time. Sometimes it means giving up something you enjoy. Fasting during Lent is a reminder of Jesus' time spent praying in the desert. How might your family practice fasting?

Ashes, Ashes

- Attend an Ash Wednesday service as a family.

- After the service, talk about what it felt like to have the ashes put on your forehead. Talk about what it feels like to remember that you are human.

Remembering Jesus' Love

- Each night for a week, sing a verse of "Jesus Loves Me" before bed.

- Talk about how it feels to know that Jesus loves you.

Fasting

SAY: Sometimes during Lent people give up something they enjoy to remind them of the time Jesus spent praying in the desert. Let's choose something we can do to help us remember.

- Choose a way to fast as a family. It can be something small, such as giving up dessert on weekdays or limiting screen time to a shorter amount per day.

Talking About Death

On Ash Wednesday and throughout Lent we are reminded that we are living humans who one day will physically die. Death and dying can be a difficult subject for all of us to talk about. It can be especially difficult to answer kids' questions.

- Read the book, *The Fall of Freddie the Leaf: A Story of Life for All Ages* by Leo Buscaglia.

- Invite your child to talk to you about their thoughts, feelings, and questions. Remember, it is OK to say, "I don't know. Let's think about it together."

Remember that you made me from clay, and you will return me to dust. (Job 10:9)

Recommended Resources for the Whole Family

Make Room: A Child's Guide to Lent and Easter, Laura Alary (Picture Book - ages 8-12)

What Is Lent? Preparing for Easter, Marcia Stoner (Pack of 5 Booklets - youth)

Waiting for Wings, Lois Elhert (Picture Book - ages 3+)

What We Do in Lent: A Child's Activity Book, Anne E. Kitch (Activity Book - family)

Ash Wednesday (Chuck Knows Church Video - appropriate for all ages but most interesting for 10+) https://chuckknowschurch.com/archive/16ash-wednesday

Lent (Chuck Knows Church Video - all ages) https://chuckknowschurch.com/archive/14lent

Holy Week and Easter

Holy Moment Activity

Supplies: crayons or markers

- Photocopy" "Holy Week" (p. 72) for each child.

SAY: Holy Week is an important time for people who follow Jesus. This is the week that we remember Jesus' last days before going to the cross and being resurrected.

- Give each child a copy of "Holy Week," and invite children to color the images. As they color, discuss the images for each day.

Holy Moment Activity

SAY: Let's share an Easter greeting. I will say, "The Lord is risen!" Then you say, "He is risen indeed!" Let's try it. The Lord is risen! **He is risen indeed!** Let's try the greeting another way. I will say, "Jesus is alive!" You say, "Yes, he is!" Jesus is alive! **Yes, he is!**

Holy Moment Activity

Supplies: Drawn or printed pictures of emojis that represent the feelings sad, confused, happy, and surprised. Tape to the walls of the room in four different areas.

SAY: The story of Easter is full of lots of different emotions. Sometimes the people in the story were sad, confused, happy, or surprised. As I tell the story, go stand next to the emoji that shows what the people might have been feeling. Listen carefully, because the feelings may change.

It had been an awful few days for Jesus' friends. Jesus had been killed on a cross and buried in a tomb. Everyone was very *sad.* The women spent time together preparing spices and perfumes to anoint Jesus' body. On the first morning of the week, the women took the spices and perfumes to the tomb. When they arrived there, they saw that the stone used to close the tomb had been rolled away and the tomb was empty. The women were so *confused!* What had happened to Jesus? Suddenly, two men wearing bright white clothes were standing by them. The women were *surprised!* The men said, "Why are you looking for Jesus here? This isn't where you find living people. Jesus isn't here. Remember, he told you this would happen." The women felt so *happy!* They went right away to tell everyone what had happened. When they got there, Jesus' friends were all very *sad.* After the women told them what happened, everyone was *surprised* and *confused.* The women's story was unbelievable! Even though Peter wasn't sure about the women's story, he ran to the tomb to see for himself. When he got to the tomb, he looked inside. To his *surprise,* the women were right. Jesus wasn't there! Peter went home *confused* but *happy* about all he had seen.

Preparing to Lead: He Is Risen!

He is risen! He is risen indeed! This paschal, or Easter, greeting is said to have begun in the early days following Jesus' resurrection. The paschal greeting is said in some variation by Christians all over the world. Does your church or family tradition have a paschal greeting?

When the women in Luke's story arrived at the tomb, and saw it was empty, two men appeared in bright clothing and delivered the first ever paschal greeting: "He isn't here, but has been raised." The women went to tell the others what I imagine was something like a paschal greeting as well: "He is risen!" Peter ran to the tomb to see for himself what had happened. Jesus wasn't there. I wonder if Peter looked at the women and responded: "He is risen indeed!"

Holy Week

 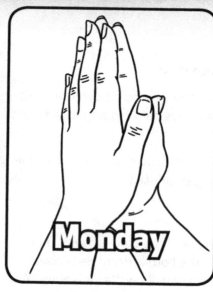 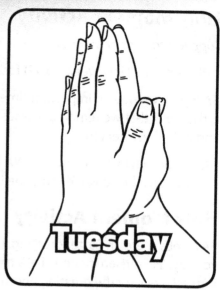

HOLY MOMENTS: Activities for
Teaching Children About Worship

Holy Moments at Home: Holy Week and Easter

Dear Parents and Caregivers,

He is risen! He is risen indeed! This paschal, or Easter, greeting is said to have begun in the early days following Jesus' resurrection. The paschal greeting is said in some variation by Christians all over the world. Does your church or family tradition have a paschal greeting?

In Luke's account, when the women arrived at the tomb and saw that it was empty, two men appeared in bright clothing and delivered the first ever paschal greeting: "He isn't here, but has been raised." The women went to tell the others what I imagine was something like a paschal greeting as well: "He is risen!" Peter ran to the tomb to see for himself what had happened. Jesus wasn't there. I wonder if Peter looked at the women and responded: "He is risen indeed!"

Quiet Friday Night

- Turn off all the noise-making electronics such as televisions, computers, and cell phones for at least one hour.

- Spend time together doing something as a family, or do quiet activities individually.

Clean and Dirty Feet

During Holy Week, Jesus washed the disciples' feet.

- Before bath time, talk about feet. Why do feet get so dirty? Why are feet important? Why did Jesus choose to wash his disciples' feet?

- After bath time, take turns putting lotion on one another's feet.

The Last Supper

- Wonder together about what Jesus' meal with his friends may have looked like.

- Using a child-safe web browser, or your local library, find art images of the Last Supper. How are they the same? How are they different?

Jesus is Alive!

- Share the good news! Use sidewalk chalk to write "Jesus is alive!" on your driveway, sidewalk, or another concrete surface. Draw pictures that remind you of new life. Invite a friend to join you.

He isn't here, because he has been raised from the dead, just as he said. Come, see the place where they laid him. (Matthew 28:6)

Recommended Resources for the Whole Family

- *Holy Week: An Emotions Primer* (Baby Believer®) Board book - Danielle Hitchen

- *Little Colt's Palm Sunday,* Michelle Abrams (Picture Book - ages 3+)

- *He Is Risen: Rocks Tell the Story of Easter,* Patti Rokus (Picture Book - all ages)

- *From a Deep Blue Night to a Bright Morning Light: An Easter Story,* Daphna Flegal (Picture Book and DVD - ages 3+)

- *Holy Week* (Chuck Knows Church Video - ages 10+) https://chuckknowschurch.com/archive/91holy-week

- *Palm Sunday* (Chuck Knows Church Video - all ages) https://chuckknowschurch.com/archive/46Palm-Sunday

- *Good Friday* (Chuck Knows Church Video - ages 10+) https://chuckknowschurch.com/archive/72Good-Friday

Pentecost

Preparing to Lead: Happy Birthday, Church!

During the festival of Pentecost, the Holy Spirit came to Jesus' followers to be a helper, just as Jesus had promised. Traditionally, we now call Pentecost the birthday of the church.

As you prepare to lead this Holy Moment Activity, think about your experience with the Holy Spirit. The Bible describes the Holy Spirit in this story as a rushing wind and flames of fire. How would you describe the Holy Spirit? How is the arrival of the Holy Spirit like the birth of the church?

Holy Moment Activity

• Sing together "Every Time I Feel the Spirit" (p. 23).

• Tell the Pentecost story below. Stop at every # symbol to sing together a chorus of "Every Time I Feel the Spirit."

SAY: Help me tell the Bible story of Pentecost. Along the way I will stop several times for us to sing about the Spirit together. #

It was the day of Pentecost, and all the disciples had gathered in one place. Suddenly, a loud noise filled the entire house. It sounded like a howling windstorm! The disciples looked at one another and saw what looked like flames of fire on each one of them. Then they were filled with the Holy Spirit, and the Holy Spirit helped them begin to speak other languages. #

There were Jewish people from every nation living in Jerusalem. They heard the sounds and all came to see what was happening. Everyone was amazed and confused because they heard the disciples speaking in languages they could understand. #

Peter stood up and began preaching to the people. He told them all about Jesus and the Holy Spirit. He said God's promise was for everyone. The people who heard Peter's message and believed were baptized. God added 3,000 people to their community of Jesus followers that day! #

Holy Moment Activity

Supplies: glue sticks, tissue paper (red, yellow, and orange), construction paper (optional)

• Photocopy of "Pentecost Flames" (p. 75) for each child.

• Give each child a copy of "Pentecost Flames" and a glue stick.

• Invite the children to tear flame-colored tissue paper into small pieces and glue them onto the paper flames to create a three-dimensional image.

Option: Cut construction paper into long, 2-inch-wide strips. Use the strips to create headbands for the children. Cut out the children's flames and attach them to their headbands for the children to wear.

Pentecost Flames

Holy Moments at Home: Pentecost

Dear Parents and Caregivers,

During the festival of Pentecost, the Holy Spirit came to Jesus' followers to be a helper, just as Jesus had promised.

Traditionally, we now call Pentecost the birthday of the church. Do you know how many candles would be on your local church's birthday cake?

The Bible describes the Holy Spirit in this story as a rushing wind and flames of fire. Think about the Holy Spirit. How would you describe the Holy Spirit? Have you ever felt God's presence as the Holy Spirit? What did it feel like? How did you know it was the Holy Spirit that you felt? Spend some time talking about these things as a family. Listen and affirm one another's ideas and feelings.

Celebration of the Spirit Collage

- Place old magazines with child-friendly images on the table.

- Look through the magazines together to find images of celebrating. Also look for images that remind you of the Holy Spirit, especially wind and flame images.

- Cut out or tear out the images and work together to create a Celebration of Spirit Collage by gluing them to a piece of construction paper.

- Hang the collage in a location where everyone in the family can see it.

Happy Birthday

SAY: Pentecost is often called the birthday of the church. It isn't just our church's birthday. It is celebrated as the birthday of all Christian churches.

- Plan a pretend birthday party. Decide together whose birthday you will celebrate. Create a pretend guest list, and don't forget to invite your favorite stuffed animals. Decorate, share a pretend birthday cake, and play party games.

Fly a Kite

- Make or purchase a kite.

- Go kite flying together.

ASK: What does flying a kite teach you about the wind? What does it teach you about the Holy Spirit?

They were all filled with the Holy Spirit and began to speak in other languages as the Spirit enabled them to speak. (Acts 2:4)

Recommended Resources for the Whole Family

- *The Day When God Made Church: A Child's First Book About Pentecost,* Rebekah McLeod Hutto (Picture Book - ages 3+)

- *Pentecost (*Chuck Knows Church Video - all ages) https://chuckknowschurch.com/archive/29Pentecost

- *40 Day with the Holy Spirit,* Jack Levison (Book - adults)

- *What Is Pentecost?* Abingdon Press (Pack of 5 Booklets - youth)

- *Acts of the Apostles: What is Pentecost? (*What's in the Bible Video - all ages) https://tinyurl.com/pentecostchurch

All Saints' Day

Preparing to Lead: Saints All Around Us

All Saints' Day is a celebration of all of the saints who have come before us. On this day we honor people who have lived lives of faith, and who have shared that faith with us.

What is a saint? Every follower of Jesus is a saint. In the Catholic church, saints are a specific group of people who meet specific qualifications. In the Protestant church, we talk about saints as all people who faithfully follow Christ. We believe in the "communion of saints," the believers of the past, present, and future. We believe that when we worship as children of God, the entire communion of saints worships with us.

On All Saints' Day we are reminded that the people we love are always with us, and that our spirits will continue to be with future saints even after we are physically gone.

As you prepare for this Holy Moment Activity, think about the saints you have known in your life. Who has made an impact on your spirit?

Holy Moment Activity

Supplies: handbell or small bell

SAY: All Saints' Day is a special day when we remember all of the Jesus followers who were here before us. We can learn so much from them! We believe that the people we love who have died are always here with us in spirit. Sometimes we call that the "communion of saints."

One way we celebrate All Saints' Day is by remembering our loved ones who have died by saying their names and ringing a bell. Today we will each have a turn to ring the bell. If someone you love has died, you may say their name before you ring the bell.

• Demonstrate by saying a name and ringing the bell.

• Allow each child to have a chance to ring the bell, even if the child does not say a name.

TIP: Be sensitive to the feelings and thoughts that come from the children during this Holy Moment Activity. Remember to acknowledge each child's thoughts and feelings with love and grace.

PRAY: Thank you, God, for all of the saints. Thank you for their lives and for the opportunity to learn from them.

Extended Discussion Question

Use this question to extend the activity for older children, youth, and adults:

ASK: How does it feel to know you are a part of the communion of saints?

Holy Moments at Home: All Saints' Day

Dear Parents and Caregivers,

All Saints' Day is a celebration of all the saints who have come before us. On this day we honor people who have lived lives of faith, and who have shared that faith with us.

In the Catholic church, saints are a specific group of people who meet specific qualifications. In the Protestant church, we talk about saints as all people who faithfully follow Christ. We believe in the "communion of saints," the believers of the past, present, and future. We believe that when we worship as children of God, the entire communion of saints worships with us. Every follower of Jesus is a saint.

On All Saints' Day we are reminded that the people we love are always with us, and that our spirits will continue to be in worship with future saints even after we are physically gone.

Who Is a Saint?

SAY: In our church, we call someone who believes in and follows Jesus a saint. Do you know any saints?

- Listen together to the song, "I Sing a Song of the Saints of God." A video version is listed in the Recommended Resources below. You can find the lyrics to the hymn here, https://www.hymnsite.com/lyrics/umh712.sht, or in the United Methodist Hymnal #712.

- Work together to name a person you know, or know about, that matches each person in the hymn. What makes them a saint?

- Write your own verse together. Where do you meet saints?

Our Family is Full of Saints

- Sit together with a large sheet of paper.

- Write the children's names at the bottom. Begin creating a family tree moving up the page by adding parents and grandparents.

- Continue to add family members until the page is full.

OPTION: Add members of your chosen family to your family tree. Talk about what makes them an important part of your family.

Dinner with Saints

- Invite two or three people who are a part of your church family to share a meal with your family at home or at a restaurant.

- Encourage the children to help choose who to invite.

So then, with endurance, let's also run the race that is laid out in front of us, since we have such a great cloud of witnesses surrounding us. (Hebrews 12:1a)

Recommended Resources for the Whole Family

- *Badger's Parting Gifts,* Susan Varley (Picture Book - ages 4+)

- *Nana Upstairs, Nana Downstairs,* Tommie dePaola (Picture Book - ages 4+, deals with death of a grandparent)

- *The Wall,* Eve Bunting (Picture Book - ages 4+)

- *Communion of Saints,* Katie Shockley (Article - adults) https://www.ministrymatters.com/all/entry/4400/communion-of-saints

- *I Sing a Song of the Saints of God* (YouTube.com Video The Children's Choir of St. John's Episcopal Church in North Haven, CT) https://tinyurl.com/saintschoir

- *Do United Methodists Believe in Saints?* (Article - youth and adults http://www.umc.org/what-we-believe/ask-the-umc-do-united-methodists-believe-in-saints)

Intergenerational Worship Using Holy Moments

Greeting

CHILD: The Lord be with you.

ALL: And also with you.

Moment of Silence

ADULT OR YOUTH: In church we make lots of noise! We sing, we pray, and we play. Sometimes though, we are quiet. God likes it when we make noise, and God likes it when we are silent. Silence, being quiet, helps us to listen. Let's practice being quiet.

- Invite everyone to be silent. Count down from 3 so that everyone knows when the time for quiet will start.
- After 5-10 seconds, count back from 3 to alert that quiet time is over.

Procession and Lighting the Candles

- Sing a hymn or song together while children, youth, or adults bring forward a Bible, a cross, and battery-operated candles (or lighters) to light the worship-space candles.
- Invite an acolyte to light the worship-space candles, or place the battery-operated candles on a table in the front of the worship space.

CHILD OR YOUTH: Thank you, God, for always being with us. Thank you for these candles that remind us you are here. Amen.

Litany

- Read together the litany prepared by the children in the Holy Moment Activity (p. 21). If possible, allow a child to lead the litany.

Praise

- Sing together "Praise the Lord" (p. 23), dancing and pointing to each body part as it is mentioned in the song.

Prayer of Illumination

CHILD: Before we read words from the Bible and hear a sermon, we say a prayer called the Prayer of Illumination. I will lead us in a prayer like that today. I will say it, then we will say it together. Dear God, help me to listen and understand.

ALL: Dear God, help me to listen and understand.

Reading the Bible

YOUTH: A reading from 1 Timothy 3:15-17.

- Read from 1 Timothy.

YOUTH: This is the word of God for the people of God.

ALL: Thanks be to God. Amen.

Singing Psalms

- Sing together "Be Strong: Psalm 27:14" to the tune of "The Bear Went Over the Mountain" (p. 23).

Testimony-Sermon

- Invite a child, youth, or adult leader to share about their favorite story from the Bible.

Prayers of the People

CHILD OR YOUTH: Today we will pray for people who we love who have experienced joy or pain this week. We will take turns saying who we would like to pray for. After each name we will say "Lord, hear our prayer." We know that God always hears our prayers.

- Allow a few moments for worshipers to mention names. After each name, say together, **"Lord, hear our prayer."**

CHILD OR YOUTH: Dear God, thank you for hearing our prayers for those we love. In Jesus' name, Amen.

Confession and Pardon

CHILD OR YOUTH: Please join me in our Prayer of Confession.

ALL: Dear God, we have made lots of mistakes. We are sorry for the times we have not done the right thing. Please forgive us. Amen.

CHILD OR YOUTH: God promises that if we tell God our mistakes and say we are sorry, we will be forgiven. God loves you, and you are forgiven! Say that with me.

ALL: God loves you, and you are forgiven!

Passing the Peace

- Turn to one another and say "Peace be with you." Respond to one another by saying "and also with you."

The Lord's Prayer or Affirmation of Faith

- Pray The Lord's Prayer or say an Affirmation of Faith together.

Praise

- Sing a hymn together or sing a song from page 23.

Benediction

CHILD OR YOUTH: A blessing from Numbers 6:24-26: "The Lord bless you and keep you. The Lord make his face shine on you and be gracious to you. The Lord lift up his face to you and grant you peace. Amen."

CPSIA information can be obtained
at www.ICGtesting.com
Printed in the USA
LVHW010009051219
639322LV00001B/1

9 781501 890895